THE DEVIL IS LUST, LIES, AND DELUSIONS; AND THE MOST HIGH IS LOVE AND TRUTH WITHOUT CONFUSION!

CHILDREN OF THE MOST HIGH:
PRISTINE YOUTH AND FAMILY SOLUTIONS, LLC.
SONS AND DAUGHTERS OF THE MOST HIGH PUBLISHERS ®

OH, GRACIOUS MOST HIGH HEAVENLY FATHER, HOLY IS YOUR NAME, YOUR WILL BE DONE NOW AND FOREVER!

By

Woodie Hughes Jr.
CEO & Founder of the Children of the Most High:
Pristine Youth and Family Solutions LLC.
Sons and Daughters of the Most High Publishers®
Mr. Hughes is a Servant of the Most High, and a Teacher
of the Most High's Doctrine.

I0165278

I

THE DEVIL IS LUST, LIES, AND DELUSIONS; AND THE MOST HIGH IS LOVE AND TRUTH WITHOUT CONFUSION!

Editor: Sons and Daughters of the Most High Editors

ISBN: 978-1-948355-02-5

Library of Congress Control Number: 2020906479

FOR MORE INFORMATION CONTACT:

Woodie Hughes Jr., CEO & Founder of the Children of the Most High: Pristine Youth and Family Solutions, LLC.
Sons and Daughters of the Most High Publishers ®
info@childrenofthemosthigh.com

Online ordering is available for all products at our Amazon Store Front on our website at: childrenofthemosthigh.com
Or, write to us at: Children of the Most High: Pristine Youth and Family Solutions, LLC. P.O. Box 6365, Warner Robins, Georgia 31095.

Table of Contents

Table of Contents

Table of Contents

V

CHILDREN OF THE MOST HIGH:
PRISTINE YOUTH AND FAMILY SOLUTIONS, LLC.
SONS AND DAUGHTERS OF THE MOST HIGH PUBLISHERS ®

OH, GRACIOUS MOST HIGH HEAVENLY FATHER, HOLY IS YOUR
NAME, YOUR WILL BE DONE NOW AND FOREVER!

Greetings:

We greet all members of humanity in peace! Nothing would
exist if you Oh Gracious Most High Heavenly Father, The
Creator didn't create it. You are alone in Your Greatness; you
have no partners that share in your grace. To you all sovereignty
is due and you are all powerful over everything. We seek refuge
in you, the ever watchful Most High who hears and knows all
things! Glory be to you as many times as the number of things
you have created! All gratitude is due to you oh gracious Most
High Heavenly Father, you are the Creator and Sustainer of all
the boundless universes. You are the Yielder, and the Most
Merciful. The Ruler of the Day of Decision. It's you whom we
worship and it is you alone whom we beseech for help, oh
Guide, guide us to the narrow path **which reflects moral
integrity and positive character traits in action** of the ones
who stand straight, the narrow path of those who earned your
grace not inclusive of those who brought an everlasting curse
on themselves, those who conceal the facts of that which they
know to be true in order to lead the **sincere-hearted seekers** of
your truth astray. Amen

1

CHILDREN OF THE MOST HIGH:
PRISTINE YOUTH AND FAMILY SOLUTIONS, LLC.
SONS AND DAUGHTERS OF THE MOST HIGH PUBLISHERS ®

OH, GRACIOUS MOST HIGH HEAVENLY FATHER, HOLY IS YOUR
NAME, YOUR WILL BE DONE NOW AND FOREVER!

What does the phrase: "those who earned your grace" mean as oppose to saying "those who receive your grace?"

The word: **"grace"** in the King James Version (KJV) bible book of Genesis chapter 6 verse 8 is: חֵן **Khane** or **chen** pronounced as **khān (KJV bible Hebrew Strong's Concordance#2580)**. The word: "חֵן **Khane** or **chen**" means **"favor, kindness."** The word: **"grace"** in the KJV bible book of John chapter 1 verse 17 is: χάρις **Kharece** or **charis** pronounced as **khä'-rēs (KJV bible Greek Strong's Concordance#5485)**. The word: "χάρις **Kharece** or **charis**" means **"joy, delight."** So, the phrase: **"those who earned your grace"** is in reference **to those people who are no longer physically alive that have transitioned to a higher life** such as: **Yashu'a (Jesus), John the Baptist, Yowkhanan Bar Zebedee (John Son of Zebedee who was Yashu'a (Jesus) beloved disciple),** or **Ab-Ra-Kham (Abraham).**

2

CHILDREN OF THE MOST HIGH:
PRISTINE YOUTH AND FAMILY SOLUTIONS, LLC.
SONS AND DAUGHTERS OF THE MOST HIGH PUBLISHERS ®

OH, GRACIOUS MOST HIGH HEAVENLY FATHER, HOLY IS YOUR
NAME, YOUR WILL BE DONE NOW AND FOREVER!

The phrase: **"those who receive your grace"** is in reference **to any person or people** who the Most High Heavenly Father bestows <u>**favor**</u> on by allowing them to still be physically alive, and to have an opportunity to experience <u>**joy**</u> while still be physically alive.

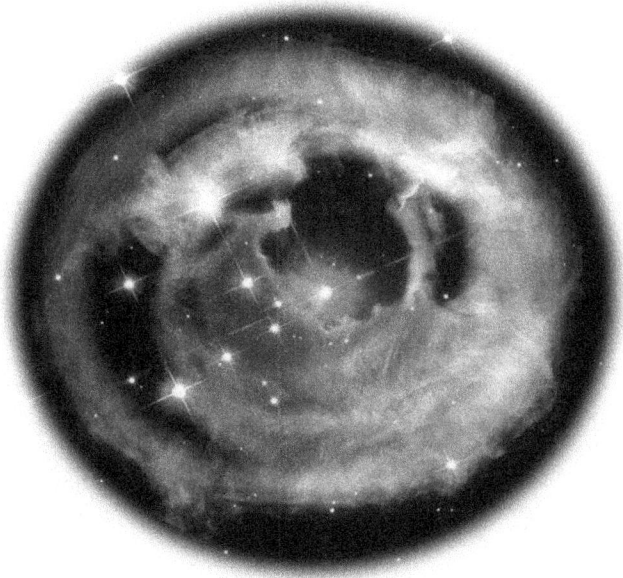

THE DEVIL IS LUST, LIES, AND DELUSIONS; AND
THE MOST IS LOVE AND TRUTH WITHOUT CONFUSION!

CHILDREN OF THE MOST HIGH:
PRISTINE YOUTH AND FAMILY SOLUTIONS, LLC.
SONS AND DAUGHTERS OF THE MOST HIGH PUBLISHERS ®

OH, GRACIOUS MOST HIGH HEAVENLY FATHER, HOLY IS YOUR
NAME, YOUR WILL BE DONE NOW AND FOREVER!

Dedication

The "The Devil is Lust, Lies and Delusion, and the Most High is Love and Truth Without Confusion!" book is dedicated to all youth and all adults who are children of the Most High that want to learn the doctrine of the **Most High** (**ELYOWN** עֶלְיוֹן) **God** (**EL** אֵל) in a way that reflects the original languages of the bible before being translated into the English language, and that reflects the original Most High Heavenly Father's doctrine that Yashu'a Ha Mashiakh (Jesus the Messiah) taught. In the KJV bible book of Genesis chapter 14 verse 18 states: "And Melchizedek king of Salem brought forth bread and wine: and he *was* the priest of the **Most High** God." The title: "**Most High**" is: the KJV bible Hebrew Strong's Concordance#**5945** for the title: "**Most High**" (**ELYOWN** עֶלְיוֹן **EL** אֵל), **which means: "Highest, Most High, Name of God, as title, The Supreme:—(Most, on) high(-er, -est), upper(-most)."**

4

CHILDREN OF THE MOST HIGH:
PRISTINE YOUTH AND FAMILY SOLUTIONS, LLC.
SONS AND DAUGHTERS OF THE MOST HIGH PUBLISHERS ®

OH, GRACIOUS MOST HIGH HEAVENLY FATHER, HOLY IS YOUR
NAME, YOUR WILL BE DONE NOW AND FOREVER!

The title: "**God**' **in this verse** is the KJV bible Hebrew Strong's Concordance#**5945** for the title: "**God**" (**EL אֵל**), **which means: "God, god, power, mighty, goodly, great, idols, might, strong, god, god-like one, mighty one, mighty men, men of rank, mighty heroes, angels, god, false god, (demons, imaginations), and mighty things in nature."**

5

THE DEVIL IS LUST, LIES, AND DELUSIONS; AND THE MOST IS LOVE AND TRUTH WITHOUT CONFUSION!

CHILDREN OF THE MOST HIGH:
PRISTINE YOUTH AND FAMILY SOLUTIONS, LLC.
SONS AND DAUGHTERS OF THE MOST HIGH PUBLISHERS ®

OH, GRACIOUS MOST HIGH HEAVENLY FATHER, HOLY IS YOUR NAME, YOUR WILL BE DONE NOW AND FOREVER!

Acknowledgements

We thank the Most High Heavenly Father who is: The Most High Heavenly One, the Sustainer, the Nourisher, the Provider of Life, and the Creator of the boundless universes, thank you for sending the Messiah Yashu'a (Jesus) who was a willing sacrifice, and for your angelic-beings that protect us, inspire us and guide us to obey you, inclusive of the Sun of Righteousness (**Shemesh** צְדָקָה pronounced **sheh'·mesh Tsĕdaqah** שֶׁמֶשׁ pronounced **tsed·ä·kä'**) who arises with healing in his wings as stated in the King James Version (KJV) bible book of **Malachi chapter 4 verse 2**, and we thank the Most High Heavenly One for life, for health and for everything else!

6

THE DEVIL IS LUST, LIES, AND DELUSIONS; AND THE MOST IS LOVE AND TRUTH WITHOUT CONFUSION!

CHILDREN OF THE MOST HIGH:
PRISTINE YOUTH AND FAMILY SOLUTIONS, LLC.
SONS AND DAUGHTERS OF THE MOST HIGH PUBLISHERS ®

OH, GRACIOUS MOST HIGH HEAVENLY FATHER, HOLY IS YOUR NAME, YOUR WILL BE DONE NOW AND FOREVER!

A Special Thank You to: My Dad (The Honorable: Mr. Woodie Hughes Sr.), and Mom (the Noble: Mrs. Annette Hughes) for accepting the Messiah Yashu'a (Jesus) and raising me and my brothers in a Godly home filled with love as they like the Messiah Yashu'a (Jesus); willingly sacrificed their youth and many worldly possessions to ensure that my brothers and I had the greatest opportunity to achieve the maximum levels of success in all areas of our lives; **thank you Mom and Dad!** A Special Thank You to: My Beloved Wife and best friend (Mrs. Tonya L. Hughes) who sacrificed her health and well-being to give birth to our children. Our children inspire me every day to keep working hard for our family and to continuously work hard to help uplift members of humanity so that we can work together to help people and the planet earth to maintain, and sustain positive health and balance for that great day, when: "Thy kingdom will come to earth as it is in heaven."

CHILDREN OF THE MOST HIGH:
PRISTINE YOUTH AND FAMILY SOLUTIONS, LLC.
SONS AND DAUGHTERS OF THE MOST HIGH PUBLISHERS ®

OH, GRACIOUS MOST HIGH HEAVENLY FATHER, HOLY IS YOUR
NAME, YOUR WILL BE DONE NOW AND FOREVER!

We also thank the many other family members, friends, colleagues, mentors, and global spiritual family who are the children of the Most High and who are in the body of Christ.

Who are the Children of the Most High Pristine Youth and Family Solutions, LLC.?

We are teachers of the doctrine of the Most High; the doctrine that the real Messiah Yashu'a (Jesus) taught. In the KJV bible book of John chapter 7 verse 16; the Messiah Yashu'a (Jesus) stated: "My doctrine isn't mine, but his that sent me." The Children of the Most High, Pristine Youth and Family Solutions, LLC. purpose is to do the Most High Heavenly Father's will only! We exist and work under the authority of the Most High Heavenly Father, who is the Creator and the Ruler of all of the boundless universes! We acknowledge the Messiah Jesus as our Savior who **we refer to** in his original Judean/Galilean Aramic (Hebrew) language birth name **Yasu'a** or **Yashu'a** (ישוע) meaning "**Savior**" and **Jesus,** who is **the**

8

CHILDREN OF THE MOST HIGH:
PRISTINE YOUTH AND FAMILY SOLUTIONS, LLC.
SONS AND DAUGHTERS OF THE MOST HIGH PUBLISHERS ®

Son of God in English. **We have accepted the Lord Jesus Christ (Yashu'a Ha Mashiakh – Jesus the Messiah or Yehoshu'a, which means Yahayyu is Salvation or Yahayyu Saves) as our Savior and we are in the Body of Christ!**

CHILDREN OF THE MOST HIGH:
PRISTINE YOUTH AND FAMILY SOLUTIONS, LLC.
SONS AND DAUGHTERS OF THE MOST HIGH PUBLISHERS ®

What is the Mission, Vision, and Motto of the Children of the Most High; Pristine Youth and Family Solutions, LLC?

The Mission is: To **inspire** and **empower** all children of the Most High to **pristinely** make the world a safe and healthy place for all members of humanity. **The Vision is**: To **create** a world that is ruled by **Love** and the "**Will**" of the Most High, void of negative emotions, greed, lusts and love of money.

9

CHILDREN OF THE MOST HIGH:
PRISTINE YOUTH AND FAMILY SOLUTIONS, LLC.
SONS AND DAUGHTERS OF THE MOST HIGH PUBLISHERS ®

OH, GRACIOUS MOST HIGH HEAVENLY FATHER, HOLY IS YOUR
NAME, YOUR WILL BE DONE NOW AND FOREVER!

According to the KJV bible book of Matthew chapter 19 verse 26, the Messiah Yashu'a (Jesus) said unto them, "With men this is impossible; but with God all things are possible." According to the KJV bible book of Philippians chapter 4 verse 13; it states: "I can do all things through Christ which strengthened me." Therefore; with God and through Christ, the children of the Most High Pristine Youth and Family Solutions, LLC. Mission and Vision can become a reality for the children of the Most High!

Motto: There is no right way to do the wrong thing!

Who is the Most High to the Children of the Most High Pristine Youth and Family Solutions, LLC.?

The Most High Heavenly Father is Love, the Sustainer, the Nourisher, the Provider of all Life, and the Omnipotent and the Omnipresent Creator of the boundless universes.

CHILDREN OF THE MOST HIGH:
PRISTINE YOUTH AND FAMILY SOLUTIONS, LLC.
SONS AND DAUGHTERS OF THE MOST HIGH PUBLISHERS ®

OH, GRACIOUS MOST HIGH HEAVENLY FATHER, HOLY IS YOUR
NAME, YOUR WILL BE DONE NOW AND FOREVER!

The Most High Heavenly Father encompasses and interpenetrates all existence inclusive of every part of nature both visible as well as invisible. Oh, Most High Heavenly Father, you are all, and there is nothing nearer to us than you; for you encompass all things! Glory be to you alone!

In the KJV bible book of John chapter 4 verse 23, the Messiah Yashu'a (Jesus) said: "God is a Spirit: and they that worship him must worship him in spirit and in truth." In the KJV bible book of Genesis, chapter 14 verse 18 states: "And Melchizedek (**Malkiy-Tsedeq**, מַלְכִּי־צֶדֶק) king of Salem brought forth bread and wine: and he was the priest of the **Most High** (ELYOWN עֶלְיוֹן) **God** (EL אֵל)."

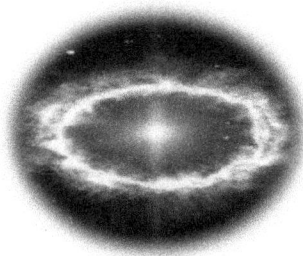

11

CHILDREN OF THE MOST HIGH:
PRISTINE YOUTH AND FAMILY SOLUTIONS, LLC.
SONS AND DAUGHTERS OF THE MOST HIGH PUBLISHERS ®

OH, GRACIOUS MOST HIGH HEAVENLY FATHER, HOLY IS YOUR
NAME, YOUR WILL BE DONE NOW AND FOREVER!

Who is the Real Messiah Jesus to the Children of the Most High Pristine Youth and Family Solutions, LLC.?

The Children of the Most High, Pristine Youth and Family Solutions, LLC., acknowledges the Real Messiah Jesus as our Savior who **we refer to** in his original Galilean/Judean Aramic (Hebrew) language, original birth name **Yasu'a (يسوع)** or **Yashu'a (ישרע)** meaning "**Savior**" also spelled Yeshua or Yehoshu'a, **Iesous** ('Ιησοῦς) in the Greek translation and as **Kurios** (Greek word for Lord), and **Issa** or **Isa** in Ashuric Syriac (Arabic). Now when **Yehoshu'a** is translated in the Hebrew language it translates as **Yahayyu Saves** or simply **Joshua**, and in the Galilean language as Yashu'a or **Yasu'a** Inar Rab (which translates as **Jesus Son of the Sustainer**), **Yashu'a Bar Yahayyu** (با حب, **Existing One**).

12

CHILDREN OF THE MOST HIGH:
PRISTINE YOUTH AND FAMILY SOLUTIONS, LLC.
SONS AND DAUGHTERS OF THE MOST HIGH PUBLISHERS ®

OH, GRACIOUS MOST HIGH HEAVENLY FATHER, HOLY IS YOUR
NAME, YOUR WILL BE DONE NOW AND FOREVER!

In Modern Hebrew translates as **Savior Son of the Everliving**
or **Savior Son of the Existing One** or **Living One**, **Yasu'** and
Haru as **Karast** "**Christ**" to the **Ancient** original indigenous
Egyptian people of what is called: "Egypt" today, not to be
confused with the Egyptians who are the nonindigenous people
who migrated to what is now known as Egypt. Yashu'a called
Jesus, is **the Son of God** in English. Yashu'a (Jesus), **the Son
of the Most High God** is the way back to the Most High. In the
KJV bible book of John chapter 14 verse 6; the Messiah
Yashu'a (Jesus) said: "I am the way, the truth, and the life:
no man (the words: "no man" is not in the original language
that this verse was revealed in. The original word for "no man"
in the Greek KJV bible translation is: "**Oudeis**" (οὐδείς, Oudeis
(is the KJV bible Greek Strong's Concordance#**3762**) means:
not one; no one, nothing. So, this phrase is inclusive of males
and females, not just males) cometh unto the Father, but by
me."

13

CHILDREN OF THE MOST HIGH:
PRISTINE YOUTH AND FAMILY SOLUTIONS, LLC.
SONS AND DAUGHTERS OF THE MOST HIGH PUBLISHERS ®

However, according to the Messiah Yashu'a (Jesus), no one can come to him unless the Most High Heavenly Father sends them to him. Yashu'a (Jesus) said in the KJV bible book of John chapter 6 verse 44: "No man (οὐδείς **oudeis**) can (δύναμαι *dynamai*) come (ἔρχομαι *erchomai*) to (πρός *pros*) me (μέ **mé, meh**), except (ἐὰν μή *ean mē*; KJV bible Greek Strong's Concordance#**3362** meaning: **if not, unless, whoever... not**) the Father which hath sent me draw (ἕλκω *helkō*; KJV bible Greek Strong's Concordance#**1670** meaning: **to draw by inward power, lead, impel; to drag (literally or figuratively)** him: and I will raise him up at the last day." Again, in the aforementioned verse, the words: "no man" is not in the original language that this verse was revealed in. The original word for "no man" is: "**Oudeis**" (οὐδείς, Oudeis (KJV bible Greek Strong's Concordance#**3762**) means: *not one; no one, nothing*.

14

CHILDREN OF THE MOST HIGH:
PRISTINE YOUTH AND FAMILY SOLUTIONS, LLC.
SONS AND DAUGHTERS OF THE MOST HIGH PUBLISHERS ®

OH, GRACIOUS MOST HIGH HEAVENLY FATHER, HOLY IS YOUR
NAME, YOUR WILL BE DONE NOW AND FOREVER!

What does the Children of the Most High Pristine Youth and Family Solutions, LLC. do?

The Children of the Most High; Pristine Youth and Family Solutions LLC. does the will of the Most High Heavenly Father. We are **Teachers** and **Administrators** of the Most High Doctrine and work diligently to teach youth and adults how to solve problems, and how to successfully work through difficult problems or issues or situations by utilizing the **Children of the Most High Pristine Youth and Family Solutions, LLC. 9X9 True Vine "Yashu'a" (Jesus) B.A. (Soul) K.A. (Spirit) R.E. (Sun) ("RE" is pronounced as "RAY") Sequential Order of Learning. More information about the True Vine "Yashu'a" (Jesus) B.A.-K.A.-R.E. Sequential Order of Learning will be expounded on in chapter 3.** Our targeted audiences are youth (who are between the 5th and 12th grades) and adults who are children of the Most High.

15

CHILDREN OF THE MOST HIGH:
PRISTINE YOUTH AND FAMILY SOLUTIONS, LLC.
SONS AND DAUGHTERS OF THE MOST HIGH PUBLISHERS ®

OH, GRACIOUS MOST HIGH HEAVENLY FATHER, HOLY IS YOUR
NAME, YOUR WILL BE DONE NOW AND FOREVER!

So, we teach in an effort to make the doctrine of the Most High clear in the minds of people who want to learn the original message or messages of the scriptures before they were translated into other languages, and we teach in an effort to create an opportunity for them to learn how to apply the doctrine of the Most High in all that they aspire to do!

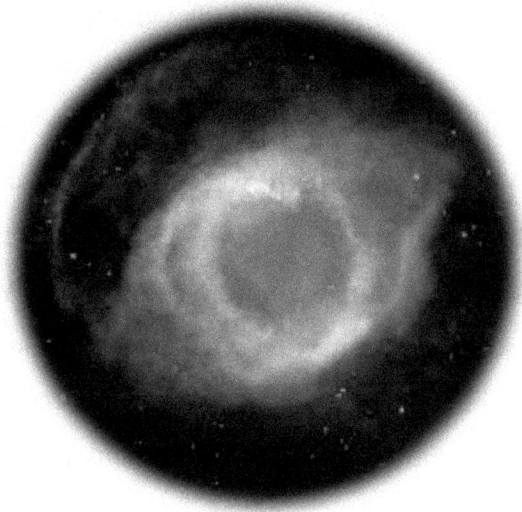

CHILDREN OF THE MOST HIGH:
PRISTINE YOUTH AND FAMILY SOLUTIONS, LLC.
SONS AND DAUGHTERS OF THE MOST HIGH PUBLISHERS ®

OH, GRACIOUS MOST HIGH HEAVENLY FATHER, HOLY IS YOUR
NAME, YOUR WILL BE DONE NOW AND FOREVER!

**Why does the Children of the Most High Pristine Youth and
Family Solutions, LLC. refer to themselves as T̲eachers /
A̲dministers of the Most High Heavenly Father's Doctrine
instead of P̲reachers?**

The Children of the Most High Pristine Youth and Family
Solutions, LLC. refer to themselves as T̲eachers and
A̲dministers of the Most High Heavenly Father's Doctrine
that Yashu'a (Jesus) taught instead of P̲reachers because the
Most High inspired and endowed them with the knowledge and
with the ability to teach with the True-Vine (Yashu'a, Jesus)
Spirit of the Word of Knowledge in the KJV bible book of 1st
Corinthians chapter 12 verse 8 to teach the Most High's
Doctrine as mentioned in the KJV bible book of John chapter 7
verse 16.

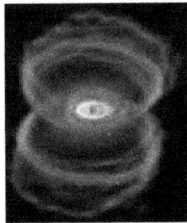

17

CHILDREN OF THE MOST HIGH:
PRISTINE YOUTH AND FAMILY SOLUTIONS, LLC.
SONS AND DAUGHTERS OF THE MOST HIGH PUBLISHERS ®

OH, GRACIOUS MOST HIGH HEAVENLY FATHER, HOLY IS YOUR
NAME, YOUR WILL BE DONE NOW AND FOREVER!

In the KJV bible book of Matthews chapter 28 verses 19-20, the Messiah Yashu'a (Jesus) said: "Go ye therefore, and teach all nations, baptizing them in the name of the Father, and of the Son, and of the Holy Ghost. Teaching them to observe all things whatsoever I have commanded you: and, lo, I am with you always, even unto the end of the world. Amen." The word in the aforementioned KJV bible book of Matthews chapter 28 verse 19 for *teach* is: the **KJV bible Greek Strong's Concordance#3100 mathēteuō (μαθητεύω) which means: teach, instruct, be disciple**. The word in the book of Matthews chapter 28 verse 20 for *Teaching* is: the **KJV bible Greek Strong's Concordance#1321 didaskō (διδάσκω) which means: to teach, to hold discourse with others in order to instruct them, deliver didactic discourses, to be a teacher, to discharge the office of a teacher, conduct one's self as a teacher, to teach one, to impart instruction, instill doctrine into one, the thing taught or enjoined, to explain or expound a thing, to teach one something.**

18

CHILDREN OF THE MOST HIGH:
PRISTINE YOUTH AND FAMILY SOLUTIONS, LLC.
SONS AND DAUGHTERS OF THE MOST HIGH PUBLISHERS ®

OH, GRACIOUS MOST HIGH HEAVENLY FATHER, HOLY IS YOUR
NAME, YOUR WILL BE DONE NOW AND FOREVER!

The word for **"Preach"** in the **KJV bible book of Matthew
chapter 11 verse 1** is: the **KJV bible Greek Strong's
Concordance#2784 kēryssō (κηρύσσω) which means to:
preach, publish, and proclaim**. In the KJV bible book of
Matthew chapter 11 verse 1; it states: "And it came to pass,
when Jesus had made an end of commanding his twelve
disciples, he departed thence to **teach** and to **preach** in their
cities. The plural noun of "**teach**" is "**Teachers**": the **KJV bible
Greek Strong's Concordance#1320 didaskalos
(διδάσκαλος,** meaning one who teaches or teachers) and has
the same root foundation as the word for "**Teach**" (the **KJV
bible Greek Strong's Concordance#1321 didaskō
(διδάσκω)** in the book of Acts chapter 13 verse 1; and states:
"Now there were in the church that was at Antioch certain
prophets and **teachers**; as Barnabas, and Simeon that was called
Niger, and Lucius of Cyrene, and Manaen, which had been
brought up with Herod the tetrarch, and Saul."

19

THE DEVIL IS LUST, LIES, AND DELUSIONS; AND
THE MOST IS LOVE AND TRUTH WITHOUT CONFUSION!

CHILDREN OF THE MOST HIGH:
PRISTINE YOUTH AND FAMILY SOLUTIONS, LLC.
SONS AND DAUGHTERS OF THE MOST HIGH PUBLISHERS ®

OH, GRACIOUS MOST HIGH HEAVENLY FATHER, HOLY IS YOUR
NAME, YOUR WILL BE DONE NOW AND FOREVER!

In the aforementioned verse, the word: **"Niger"** is the **KJV Bible Greek Strong's Concordance#3526 Νίγερ (Niger)** which means: **Νίγερ Níger, neeg'-er**; **of Latin origin**; **black**; **Niger, a Christian**: **Niger**. According to the African American Registry (2019): "The history of the word **nigger is often traced to the Latin word Niger**, **meaning Black**. This word became the noun, Negro (Black person) in English." The KJV bible book of Hosea, chapter 4 verse 6; states: "My people are destroyed for lack of knowledge: because thou hast rejected knowledge, I will also reject thee, that thou shalt be no priest to me: seeing thou hast forgotten the law of thy God, I will also forget thy children." The KJV bible book of Isaiah, chapter 5 verse 13; states: "Therefore my people are gone into captivity, because they have no knowledge: and their honorable men are famished, and their multitude dried up with thirst."

THE DEVIL IS LUST, LIES, AND DELUSIONS; AND
THE MOST IS LOVE AND TRUTH WITHOUT CONFUSION!

CHILDREN OF THE MOST HIGH:
PRISTINE YOUTH AND FAMILY SOLUTIONS, LLC.
SONS AND DAUGHTERS OF THE MOST HIGH PUBLISHERS ®

OH, GRACIOUS MOST HIGH HEAVENLY FATHER, HOLY IS YOUR
NAME, YOUR WILL BE DONE NOW AND FOREVER!

So, the Children of the Most High Pristine Youth and Family Solutions, LLC. refer to themselves as **Teachers** instead of **Preachers** because after over 25 years of teaching and studying the scriptures in the languages that they were originally revealed in, the children of the Most High don't find themselves **preaching**, they found themselves **teaching**. According to the Online American Heritage Dictionary, **teaching means; instructing, explaining, and elaborating**. So, we **teach** in an effort to ensure that the children of the Most High do their best to make the doctrine of the Most High clear in the minds of people who want to learn the original message or messages of the scriptures before they were translated into other languages. According to the Online American Heritage Dictionary (2020), **Administer** is defined as:

ad·min·is·ter (ăd-mĭn′ĭ-stər)

v. **ad·min·is·tered, ad·min·is·ter·ing, ad·min·is·ters**

v.tr.

1. To have charge of; manage.

21

CHILDREN OF THE MOST HIGH:
PRISTINE YOUTH AND FAMILY SOLUTIONS, LLC.
SONS AND DAUGHTERS OF THE MOST HIGH PUBLISHERS ®

OH, GRACIOUS MOST HIGH HEAVENLY FATHER, HOLY IS YOUR
NAME, YOUR WILL BE DONE NOW AND FOREVER!

2.a. To apply as a remedy: *administer a sedative.* **1.** To manage as an administrator. **2.** To minister: *administering to their every whim.* [Middle English *administren,* from Old French *administrer,* from Latin *administrāre* : *ad,* ad- + *ministrāre,* to manage (from *minister, ministr-,* servant; see MINISTER).] So, we are "**Administers of the Most High's Doctrine**" by way of the Most High Heavenly Father giving the Children of the Most High: Pristine Youth and Family Solutions, LLC. **charge of managing the administering** of his Doctrine to inspire and empower all children of the Most High to pristinely make the world a safe and healthy place for all members of humanity. Which occurs by **applying** the Doctrine of the Most High **as a remedy** to create a world that is ruled by Love and the "Will" of the Most High, void of negative emotions, greed, lusts and love of money.

CHILDREN OF THE MOST HIGH:
PRISTINE YOUTH AND FAMILY SOLUTIONS, LLC.
SONS AND DAUGHTERS OF THE MOST HIGH PUBLISHERS ®

OH, GRACIOUS MOST HIGH HEAVENLY FATHER, HOLY IS YOUR
NAME, YOUR WILL BE DONE NOW AND FOREVER!

Why does the work that the Children of the Most High Pristine Youth and Family Solutions, LLC. do Matter? In order for the Children of the Most High; Pristine Youth and Family Solutions LLC. to be obedient to the Most High Heavenly Father, we seek to be positive difference makers who helps and teach youth and adults how to apply the doctrine of the Most High through the **True Vine "Yashu'a" (Jesus) B.A.-K.A.-R.E. Sequential Order of Learning** to teach them how to create positive predetermined goals, how to achieve positive success according to what positive success means to them, how to achieve positive happiness according to what positive happiness means to them, and how to learn to work together with members of humanity to create a world where all youth and all adults are happy, healthy, and balanced mentally, spiritually, physically, emotionally, financially, personally, professionally, and socially. "Happiness is associated with and precedes numerous successful outcomes, as well as behaviors paralleling success, Lyubomirsky, King, & Diener, (2005).

23

CHILDREN OF THE MOST HIGH:
PRISTINE YOUTH AND FAMILY SOLUTIONS, LLC.
SONS AND DAUGHTERS OF THE MOST HIGH PUBLISHERS ®

Furthermore, the evidence suggests that positive affect is the hallmark of well-being and may be the cause of many of the desirable characteristics, resources, and successes correlated with happiness, (Lyubomirsky, King, & Diener, (2005)." It also matters for our youth to receive the protection from the Most High Heavenly Father from all harm during the pre-adult years and beyond, in order to have an opportunity to become adults that can continue to create a world where all youth and all adults are happy, healthy, and balanced mentally, spiritually, physically, emotionally, financially, personally, professionally, and socially. According the bible, this can only occur if our youth learn God's knowledge and obey God's laws. According to the KJV bible book of Hosea chapter 4 verse 6, the LORD states: **"My people are destroyed for lack of knowledge**: because thou hast rejected knowledge, I will also reject thee, that thou shalt be no priest to me: **seeing thou hast forgotten the law of thy God, I will also forget thy children**."

24

CHILDREN OF THE MOST HIGH:
PRISTINE YOUTH AND FAMILY SOLUTIONS, LLC.
SONS AND DAUGHTERS OF THE MOST HIGH PUBLISHERS ®

OH, GRACIOUS MOST HIGH HEAVENLY FATHER, HOLY IS YOUR
NAME, YOUR WILL BE DONE NOW AND FOREVER!

So, according to the aforementioned verse, in order to best prepare today's youth to survive and thrive until adulthood and beyond, they need to learn **God's (אלהים Elôhîym)** knowledge **(Elôhîym, אלהים is the original word for "God" before being translated as the word: "God" in the KJV bible book of Genesis chapter 1 verse 1)**, and **God's (אלהים Elôhîym)** laws to be eligible to receive **God's (אלהים Elôhîym)** protection from all harm.

My Shield is God Most High
Who saves the upright in heart.
Psalm 7:10

25

CHILDREN OF THE MOST HIGH:
PRISTINE YOUTH AND FAMILY SOLUTIONS, LLC.
SONS AND DAUGHTERS OF THE MOST HIGH PUBLISHERS ®

OH, GRACIOUS MOST HIGH HEAVENLY FATHER, HOLY IS YOUR
NAME, YOUR WILL BE DONE NOW AND FOREVER!

Therefore, today's youth must be informed with **God's (אלהים**
Elôhîym) All, Wise, Abundant, Right, Exact (A.W.A.R.E.)
Knowledge. How do you know? Because God's **A.W.A.R.E.**
knowledge is **best**, **accurate**, **correct** (**right, healthy**) and
exact and best to guide and protect all of the global children of
the Most High from all harm. For this reason, **God's (אלהים**
Elôhîym) A.W.A.R.E. Knowledge gives the children of the
Most High the ability to develop the habit of **positive thinking**
or correct (**right, healthy) thinking** as oppose to **negative**
thinking or **wrong thinking**. A person with **wrong knowledge**
thinks negatively by having **wrong I. D. E. A. S.** (**I**mpure
Desires **E**motionally **A**ctivated **S**equentially) or negative
thoughts continuously, which leads to negative thinking,
negative speaking, negative actions, and negative character.
Learning, applying and obeying the laws of Elohiym (God),
activates the will of the Most High Heavenly Father in the
mind which initiates all thoughts, and a person acts and
speaks, as he or she thinks!

26

THE DEVIL IS LUST, LIES, AND DELUSIONS; AND
THE MOST IS LOVE AND TRUTH WITHOUT CONFUSION!

CHILDREN OF THE MOST HIGH:
PRISTINE YOUTH AND FAMILY SOLUTIONS, LLC.
SONS AND DAUGHTERS OF THE MOST HIGH PUBLISHERS ®

OH, GRACIOUS MOST HIGH HEAVENLY FATHER, HOLY IS YOUR
NAME, YOUR WILL BE DONE NOW AND FOREVER!

This is why in the KJV bible book of Hebrews chapter 8 verse
10; it states: "For this is the covenant that I will make with the
house of Israel after those days, saith the Lord; **I will put my
laws into their mind, and write them in their hearts**: and I
will be to them a God, and they shall be to me a people."

27

CHILDREN OF THE MOST HIGH:
PRISTINE YOUTH AND FAMILY SOLUTIONS, LLC.
SONS AND DAUGHTERS OF THE MOST HIGH PUBLISHERS ®

OH, GRACIOUS MOST HIGH HEAVENLY FATHER, HOLY IS YOUR NAME, YOUR WILL BE DONE NOW AND FOREVER!

In the KJV bible book of Revelation chapter 22 verses 12-16; Yashu'a (Jesus) stated: "And, behold, I come quickly; and my reward is with me, to give every man according as his work shall be. I am Alpha and Omega, the beginning and the end, the first and the last. Blessed are they that do his [the Most High, Heavenly Father's, **ELYOWN** עֶלְיוֹן **EL** אֵל] commandments, that they may have right to the tree of life, and may enter in through the gates into the city. For without are dogs, and sorcerers, and whoremongers, and murderers, and idolaters, and whosoever loveth and maketh a lie. I Jesus [Yashu'a] have sent mine angel to testify unto you these things in the churches. I am the root and the offspring of David, and the bright and morning star."

28

CHILDREN OF THE MOST HIGH:
PRISTINE YOUTH AND FAMILY SOLUTIONS, LLC.
SONS AND DAUGHTERS OF THE MOST HIGH PUBLISHERS ®

OH, GRACIOUS MOST HIGH HEAVENLY FATHER, HOLY IS YOUR
NAME, YOUR WILL BE DONE NOW AND FOREVER!

Hence, **God's** (אלהים **Elôhîym**) **A.W.A.R.E. Knowledge** is the **best knowledge** for our youth to be taught in order for them to have the best opportunity to be recipients of **Elohiym** (God's) protection, and to help ensure that our youth will become the future positive leaders of tomorrow, today!

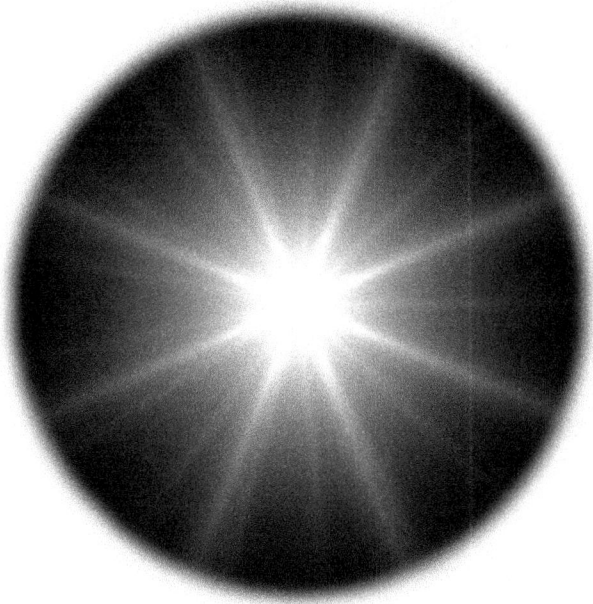

29

THE DEVIL IS LUST, LIES, AND DELUSIONS; AND
THE MOST IS LOVE AND TRUTH WITHOUT CONFUSION!

CHILDREN OF THE MOST HIGH:
PRISTINE YOUTH AND FAMILY SOLUTIONS, LLC.
SONS AND DAUGHTERS OF THE MOST HIGH PUBLISHERS ®

OH, GRACIOUS MOST HIGH HEAVENLY FATHER, HOLY IS YOUR
NAME, YOUR WILL BE DONE NOW AND FOREVER!

Chapter 1: The Most High is Love and Truth Without Confusion!

The Messiah Yashu'a (Jesus) said: "Father, if thou be willing, remove this cup from me: nevertheless, not my will, but thine, be done."
(KJV bible book of Luke chapter 22 verse 44).

30

THE DEVIL IS LUST, LIES, AND DELUSIONS; AND THE MOST IS LOVE AND TRUTH WITHOUT CONFUSION!

CHILDREN OF THE MOST HIGH:
PRISTINE YOUTH AND FAMILY SOLUTIONS, LLC.
SONS AND DAUGHTERS OF THE MOST HIGH PUBLISHERS ®

OH, GRACIOUS MOST HIGH HEAVENLY FATHER, HOLY IS YOUR NAME, YOUR WILL BE DONE NOW AND FOREVER!

The Children of the Most High: Pristine Youth and Family Solutions, LLC. is putting forth this book entitled: "The Devil is Lust, Lies, and Delusions; and the Most High is Love and Truth Without Confusion!" By the will of the Most High Heavenly Father to **inspire ALL youth and ALL adults who are children of the Most High** to not be deceived by the devil's lust, lies and delusions while simultaneously being empowered, inspired, and guided from moment to moment by the Most High's love and truth without confusion!

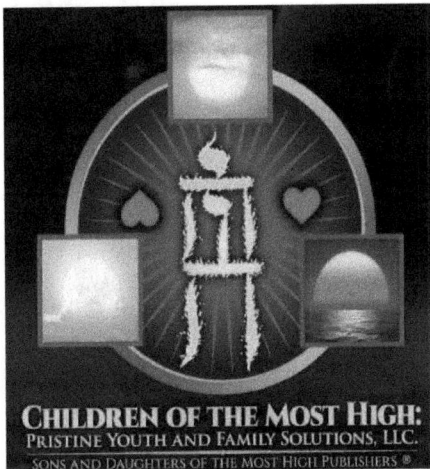

CHILDREN OF THE MOST HIGH:
PRISTINE YOUTH AND FAMILY SOLUTIONS, LLC.
SONS AND DAUGHTERS OF THE MOST HIGH PUBLISHERS ®

31

CHILDREN OF THE MOST HIGH:
PRISTINE YOUTH AND FAMILY SOLUTIONS, LLC.
SONS AND DAUGHTERS OF THE MOST HIGH PUBLISHERS ®

OH, GRACIOUS MOST HIGH HEAVENLY FATHER, HOLY IS YOUR
NAME, YOUR WILL BE DONE NOW AND FOREVER!

In the Messiah Yashu'a (Jesus) **bible book of Revelation** chapter 3 verse 20; the Messiah Yashu'a **(Jesus) said:** "Behold, I stand at the door (**of your heart,** KJV bible Greek **Strong's Concordance word#2374,** θύρα **thýra, thoo'-rah**; which is: a **door**; a **portal or entrance** (**the opening** or the closure, literally or figuratively):—**door, gate**) and knock: if any man [ἄνθρωπος **anthrōpos,** KJV bible Greek Strong's Concordance word#**444, which is a male or female human being**] hear my voice, and open the door [**of their heart**], I will come in to him [**or her**], and will sup with him [**or her**], and he [**or she**] with me."

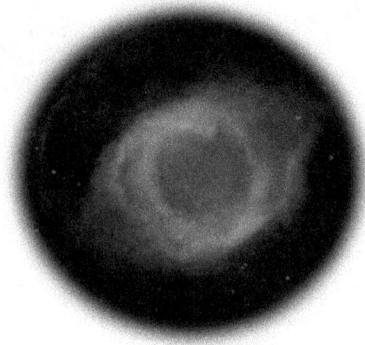

32

CHILDREN OF THE MOST HIGH:
PRISTINE YOUTH AND FAMILY SOLUTIONS, LLC.
SONS AND DAUGHTERS OF THE MOST HIGH PUBLISHERS ®

OH, GRACIOUS MOST HIGH HEAVENLY FATHER, HOLY IS YOUR
NAME, YOUR WILL BE DONE NOW AND FOREVER!

On the previous page, when you said: "In the Messiah Yashu'a **(Jesus) bible book of Revelation," are you saying that Jesus has his own book in the bible?** In the KJV bible book of Revelation chapter 1 verses 1-3; it states: "**The Revelation of Jesus Christ, which God (θεός Theos) gave unto him,** to shew unto his servants' things which must shortly come to pass; and **he sent and signified** *it* **by his angel** unto his servant John. Who bare record of the word of God, and of the testimony of Jesus Christ, and of all things that he saw. Blessed *is* he that readeth, and they that hear the words of this prophecy, and keep those things which are written therein: **for the time** *is* **at hand**." So, according to KJV book of Revelation chapter 1 verse 1, the book of Revelation is Jesus book. This is confirmed by the statement of: "**The Revelation of Jesus Christ, which God gave unto him.**" So, the answer to the question is: **YES!** according the word of God (θεός **Theos**), God (θεός **Theos**) gave the book of Revelation to the Messiah Yashu'a (Jesus).

33

CHILDREN OF THE MOST HIGH:
PRISTINE YOUTH AND FAMILY SOLUTIONS, LLC.
SONS AND DAUGHTERS OF THE MOST HIGH PUBLISHERS ®

In the KJV bible book of Matthew chapter 24 verses 4-5; the Messiah Yashu'a (Jesus) said: "Take heed that no man [ἄνθρωπος **anthrōpos,** KJV bible Greek Strong's Concordance word#**444, which is male or female human being**] deceive you. For many shall come in my name, saying, I am Christ; and shall deceive many." Therefore; In the KJV bible book of Revelation chapter 2 verse 8; the Messiah Yashu'a (Jesus) said: "And unto the angel of the church in Smyrna write; These things saith the first and the last, which was dead, and is alive."

34

CHILDREN OF THE MOST HIGH:
PRISTINE YOUTH AND FAMILY SOLUTIONS, LLC.
SONS AND DAUGHTERS OF THE MOST HIGH PUBLISHERS ®

OH, GRACIOUS MOST HIGH HEAVENLY FATHER, HOLY IS YOUR
NAME, YOUR WILL BE DONE NOW AND FOREVER!

In the KJV bible book of John chapter 15 verse 13 with KJV bible Greek Inserts, the Messiah Yashu'a (Jesus) said:

John **15:13** μείζονα ταύτης ἀγάπην οὐδεὶς ἔχει ἵνα τις τὴν ψυχὴν αὐτοῦ θῇ ὑπὲρ τῶν φίλων αὐτοῦ

"Greater love hath no man **[the Greek word for "man" in this verse is the KJV bible Greek Strong's Concordance is: οὐδείς oudeis – means a male or female human being]** than this, that a man **[οὐδείς oudeis – a male or female human being]** lay down his life for his friends." Instead of taking innocent people lives and suicide; **obedient children of the Most High must be willing to sacrifice through our sincere-hearted commitment to the service of the Most High Heavenly Father NOW and FOREVER!**

CHILDREN OF THE MOST HIGH:
PRISTINE YOUTH AND FAMILY SOLUTIONS, LLC.
SONS AND DAUGHTERS OF THE MOST HIGH PUBLISHERS ®

OH, GRACIOUS MOST HIGH HEAVENLY FATHER, HOLY IS YOUR NAME, YOUR WILL BE DONE NOW AND FOREVER!

To do so, leads to a child of the Most High taking an inner journey on the narrow path that leads to devoting our lives **to the eternal work and eternal service of the Most High Heavenly Father NOW and FOREVER! How?** By becoming consciously aware that there is more to our existence than the physical world, and more to life than all of the things that money can buy! Just by the mere fact that all that was created, was created by either creators and/or a creator that existed prior to all creation! The children of the Most High are part of creation; a portion of the Most High Heavenly Father, the Creator of all of the Boundless Universes, exists within each of the children of the Most High. However; it is up to each child of the Most High as to whether or not he or she will utilize their **"will"** to seek essential guidance from the Most High as a request to become aware of their preordained purpose and work intentionally, and consistently; moment to moment each day to fulfill their Most High Heavenly Father's; preordained purpose for their lives!

So, our desires and discipline influences how we utilize our "**will**" to make moment to moment decisions, which occurs in what the Children of the Most High: Pristine Youth and Family Solutions, LLC. refer to as the: "**Creative Garden of 'Will' (Your Mind)**." Moment to moment discipline in the obedient service to the Most High Heavenly Father's will; is an essential element in overcoming and in resisting the temptations of the **9 Deadly Venoms of the Desires of the great dragon, that old serpent called the devil and satan which deceiveth the whole world**. Therefore, if we discipline ourselves to learn and apply God's (אלהים Elôhîym) <u>A</u>ll <u>W</u>ise <u>A</u>bundant <u>R</u>ight <u>E</u>xact **(A.W.A.R.E)** Knowledge, we will reap the benefit of acquiring the ability to develop the habit of **positive thinking, if we willingly and consistently, initiate active discipline in obeying the commandments of God (אלהים Elôhîym)**.

37

THE DEVIL IS LUST, LIES, AND DELUSIONS; AND
THE MOST IS LOVE AND TRUTH WITHOUT CONFUSION!

CHILDREN OF THE MOST HIGH:
PRISTINE YOUTH AND FAMILY SOLUTIONS, LLC.
SONS AND DAUGHTERS OF THE MOST HIGH PUBLISHERS ®

OH, GRACIOUS MOST HIGH HEAVENLY FATHER, HOLY IS YOUR
NAME, YOUR WILL BE DONE NOW AND FOREVER!

Thereby, activating the "**Will**" of the Most High Heavenly
Father in our **Creative Garden of Will (Your Mind) which
initiates all thoughts and all actions. The way that a person
acts and speaks is a reflection of how he or she thinks**! A
person who utilizes **incorrect** or **wicked** or **wrong knowledge**;
thinks negatively by having wrong **I. D. E. A. S. (I**mpure
Desires **E**motionally **A**ctivated **S**equentially) or negative
thoughts continuously, which leads to negative speaking, and
negative actions.

You are free to choose,
but you are not free from
the consequences of your choice!

38

It is not possible to maintain and sustain being obedient to the Most High Heavenly Father without being intentionally disciplined to do so. It's like a person who is physically out shape and who has not ever worked out in their life; trying to do a three-day triathlon. Is that out of shape person prepared to do a three-day triathlon?

A diamond is just a piece of charcoal that handled stress exceptionally well.

Of course not, just like if an out of shape person is not fit to do a triathlon, a child of the Most High who does not diligently work to improve themselves each day; is not prepared to begin their inner journey of fulfilling their Most High preordained purpose that proceeds them.

39

THE DEVIL IS LUST, LIES, AND DELUSIONS; AND THE MOST IS LOVE AND TRUTH WITHOUT CONFUSION!

CHILDREN OF THE MOST HIGH:
PRISTINE YOUTH AND FAMILY SOLUTIONS, LLC.
SONS AND DAUGHTERS OF THE MOST HIGH PUBLISHERS ®

OH, GRACIOUS MOST HIGH HEAVENLY FATHER, HOLY IS YOUR NAME, YOUR WILL BE DONE NOW AND FOREVER!

So, whether it is in reference to physical discipline, spiritual discipline, or mental discipline; proper preparation is essential. Preparation for a child of the Most High to begin his or her inner journey of fulfilling their Most High preordained purpose, is rooted in the desire to only do the will of the Most High Heavenly Father.

In life, what can you ask for but to be real; to fulfill your potential instead of wasting energy on actualizing your dissipating image, which is not real and means expending your vital energy.

40

THE DEVIL IS LUST, LIES, AND DELUSIONS; AND
THE MOST IS LOVE AND TRUTH WITHOUT CONFUSION!

CHILDREN OF THE MOST HIGH:
PRISTINE YOUTH AND FAMILY SOLUTIONS, LLC.
SONS AND DAUGHTERS OF THE MOST HIGH PUBLISHERS ®

OH, GRACIOUS MOST HIGH HEAVENLY FATHER, HOLY IS YOUR
NAME, YOUR WILL BE DONE NOW AND FOREVER!

This is initiated through discipline of voluntary utilization of one's **"will"**, and activated **"Spiritual Majesty"** that is inspired, empowered, influenced and embraced through **"Divine Love"** for the **Most High Heavenly Father only**, and through our love for **Yasu'a** or **Yashu'a** (שׁוּעַ) meaning **"Savior"** also called **Jesus Christ. Yashu'a Ha Mashiakh (Jesus the Messiah or Yehoshu'a – Yahayyu is Salvation or Yahayyu Saves),** who is **the Son of God** in English. There is a portion of the Most High Heavenly Father which is a: **"Spiritual Majesty"** that exists in each person that is dormant in many of us and it awaits for us to utilize the **"will"** that the Most High Heavenly Father instilled in us to invoke the portion of the Most High Heavenly Father in us through **"Divine Love"** for the Most High. Positive thinking and the perpetual habit of only allowing positive thoughts to exists and flow through our minds, leads to the children of the Most High experiencing how the Most High is Love and Truth Without Confusion!

41

CHILDREN OF THE MOST HIGH:
PRISTINE YOUTH AND FAMILY SOLUTIONS, LLC.
SONS AND DAUGHTERS OF THE MOST HIGH PUBLISHERS ®

This allows us the opportunity to exercise our will to express divine love for the Most High through the '**Spiritual Majesty**' that exists in each of us!

What is "**Divine Love**", "**Spiritual Majesty**" and "**Will**"?

"**Divine Love (ISHQ)**" is a spiritual love, affection, passion for the Most High only that is from the Most High. There are various forms of love, however "**Divine Love (ISHQ)**" **is for the Most High only**!

The Dalai Lama, when asked what surprised him most about humanity, answered "Man. Because he sacrifices his health in order to make money. Then he sacrifices money to recuperate his health. And then he is so anxious about the future that he does not enjoy the present; the result being that he does not live in the present or the future; he lives as if he is never going to die, and then dies having never really lived."

42

CHILDREN OF THE MOST HIGH:
PRISTINE YOUTH AND FAMILY SOLUTIONS, LLC.
SONS AND DAUGHTERS OF THE MOST HIGH PUBLISHERS ®

OH, GRACIOUS MOST HIGH HEAVENLY FATHER, HOLY IS YOUR
NAME, YOUR WILL BE DONE NOW AND FOREVER!

**How can a portion of the Most High be in a person and a
person not know that it exists within him or her?**

In the KJV bible book of John chapter 1 verses 1-5; answers that
question for us. The KJV bible book of John chapter 1 verses 1-
5; states: "In the beginning was the Word, and the Word was
with God, and the Word was God. The same was in the
beginning with God. All things were made by him; and without
him was not anything made that was made. In him was life
(breath of life from the Lord God); and the life (**from the
Lord God made people into living souls**) was the light
(**Neshamaw Khayyeem** נשמה חיים **- Divine Breath of Life**) of
<u>men</u> (meaning **human beings**). The **KJV bible Hebrew
Strong's Concordance#444** word for "men" is: ἄνθρωπος
anthrōpos which means a human being)."

43

CHILDREN OF THE MOST HIGH:
PRISTINE YOUTH AND FAMILY SOLUTIONS, LLC.
SONS AND DAUGHTERS OF THE MOST HIGH PUBLISHERS ®

OH, GRACIOUS MOST HIGH HEAVENLY FATHER, HOLY IS YOUR NAME, YOUR WILL BE DONE NOW AND FOREVER!

"And the light (**portion of the Most High that exists in every person**) shineth in darkness (**is inside the body of every person**); and the darkness (**the body and the mind in many people who lack of the knowledge of how a portion of the Most High exists in every person**) comprehended it not.

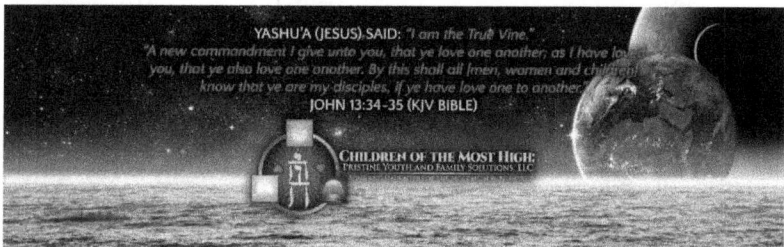

So, there is a portion of the Most High Heavenly Father which is a: "**Spiritual Majesty**" that exists in each person that is dormant in many of us. How did <u>the light shineth in darkness; and the darkness comprehended it not</u> get inside of us? The KJV bible book of **Genesis chapter 2 verse 7** answers that question; it states: "And the Lord God formed man of the dust of the ground, and breathed into his nostrils the breath of life; and man became a living soul."

44

THE DEVIL IS LUST, LIES, AND DELUSIONS; AND
THE MOST IS LOVE AND TRUTH WITHOUT CONFUSION!

CHILDREN OF THE MOST HIGH:
PRISTINE YOUTH AND FAMILY SOLUTIONS, LLC.
SONS AND DAUGHTERS OF THE MOST HIGH PUBLISHERS ®

OH, GRACIOUS MOST HIGH HEAVENLY FATHER, HOLY IS YOUR
NAME, YOUR WILL BE DONE NOW AND FOREVER!

So, according to the previous bible verse, the connection occurred when the **Yehovah (LORD) Elohiym (God)** breathed the **Khay** or **Hayy (Neshamaw Khayyeem** נשמה חיים **- Divine Breath of Life)** into the nostrils of **אָדָם 'Adam** (the **KJV bible Hebrew Strong's Concordance#120** word **"Adam"** means **a human being**) and Adam became a **Nephesh Khay** which in the Aramic (Hebrew) language, **Nephesh** is "Spirit" and **Rooahk** or **Ruwach** is "Soul". **Why are the words spirit and soul so confusing to differentiate in the English language? The words spirit and soul are confusing to differentiate in the English language** because the words **Nephesh** is "Spirit" and **Rooahk** or **Ruwah** "Soul" and **mind** are sometimes interchangeably translated in English as the same words. For example: in the KJV bible book of Genesis chapter 1:1, the Aramic (Hebrew) language word **Rooahk** or **Ruwah** "Soul" is translated in English as "**spirit**" and in Genesis (KJV) chapter 2:7, the Aramic (Hebrew) language word **Nephesh** which is "**Spirit**" is translated in English as "**Soul**".

45

THE DEVIL IS LUST, LIES, AND DELUSIONS; AND THE MOST IS LOVE AND TRUTH WITHOUT CONFUSION!

CHILDREN OF THE MOST HIGH:
PRISTINE YOUTH AND FAMILY SOLUTIONS, LLC.
SONS AND DAUGHTERS OF THE MOST HIGH PUBLISHERS ®

OH, GRACIOUS MOST HIGH HEAVENLY FATHER, HOLY IS YOUR NAME, YOUR WILL BE DONE NOW AND FOREVER!

Genesis (KJV) Chapter 1:1

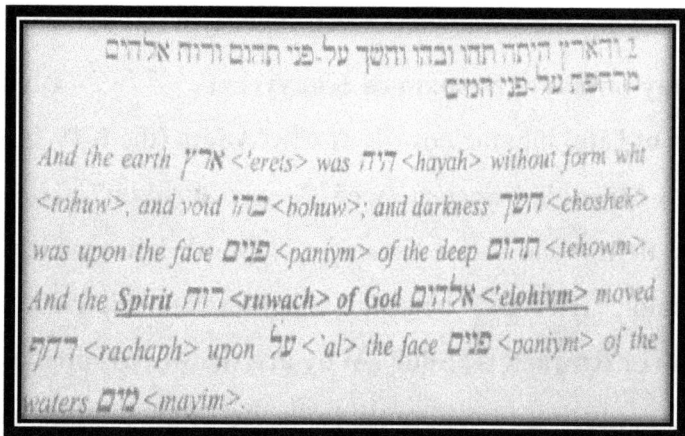

ב וְהָאָרֶץ הָיְתָה תֹהוּ וָבֹהוּ וְחֹשֶׁךְ עַל-פְּנֵי תְהוֹם וְרוּחַ אֱלֹהִים מְרַחֶפֶת עַל-פְּנֵי הַמָּיִם

And the earth אֶרֶץ <'erets> was הָיָה <hayah> without form wht <tohuw>, and void בֹּהוּ <bohuw>; and darkness חֹשֶׁךְ <choshek> was upon the face פָּנִים <panıym> of the deep תְהוֹם <tehowm>. And the Spirit רוּחַ <ruwach> of God אֱלֹהִים <'elohıym> moved רָחַף <rachaph> upon עַל <'al> the face פָּנִים <panıym> of the waters מַיִם <mayim>.

Genesis (KJV) 2:7

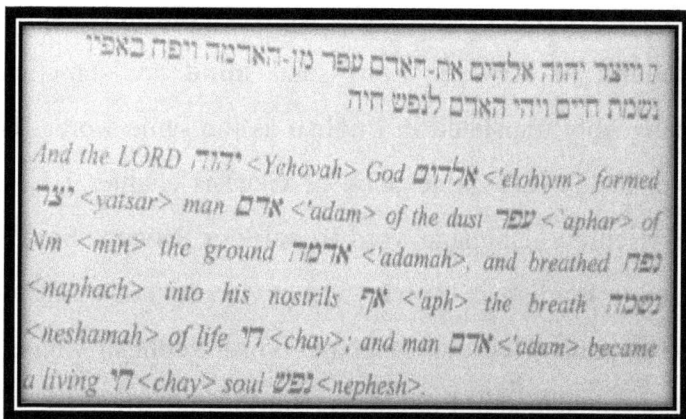

ז וַיִּיצֶר יְהוָה אֱלֹהִים אֶת-הָאָדָם עָפָר מִן-הָאֲדָמָה וַיִּפַּח בְּאַפָּיו נִשְׁמַת חַיִּים וַיְהִי הָאָדָם לְנֶפֶשׁ חַיָּה

And the LORD יְהוָה <Yehovah> God אֱלֹהִים <'elohıym> formed יָצַר <yatsar> man אָדָם <'adam> of the dust עָפָר <'aphar> of Nm <mın> the ground אֲדָמָה <'adamah>, and breathed נָפַח <naphach> into his nostrils אַף <'aph> the breath נְשָׁמָה <neshamah> of life חַי <chay>; and man אָדָם <'adam> became a living חַי <chay> soul נֶפֶשׁ <nephesh>.

46

CHILDREN OF THE MOST HIGH:
PRISTINE YOUTH AND FAMILY SOLUTIONS, LLC.
SONS AND DAUGHTERS OF THE MOST HIGH PUBLISHERS ®

OH, GRACIOUS MOST HIGH HEAVENLY FATHER, HOLY IS YOUR
NAME, YOUR WILL BE DONE NOW AND FOREVER!

What is "**Spiritual Majesty**"?

Spiritual Majesty is a portion of the Most High that exists in each person which is an inner quality that when it is intentionally organized and directed towards positive accomplishments, it activates our higher potential that helps us to conquer adverse situations. Unfortunately, **Spiritual Majesty** is usually not allowed to function in our lives due to many of us living most days according to people, places and worldly things; and other people plans for our lives that may not have our best interest; rather than becoming aware of the preordained Most High's plan for each of our lives and learning to only live in the world, but not of the world by the "**Will**" and commandments of the Most High.

CHILDREN OF THE MOST HIGH:
PRISTINE YOUTH AND FAMILY SOLUTIONS, LLC.
SONS AND DAUGHTERS OF THE MOST HIGH PUBLISHERS ®

OH, GRACIOUS MOST HIGH HEAVENLY FATHER, HOLY IS YOUR
NAME, YOUR WILL BE DONE NOW AND FOREVER!

When our **Spiritual Majesty** is intentionally organized and directed towards positive accomplishments, **it activates the ability to create positive life achievements** that afford us the opportunity **to get more out of life** by sacrificing of ourselves in a positive healthy manner **to give more to life** through our works.

What is "**Will**"? The word for "**Will**" in **Galilean Ashuric/Syriac (Arabic)** is: "**Mashiyya**".

Mashiyya (مشية) Which Comes From The Root Word Shayaa-A (شاء) Or Yashaa-A (يشاء) And Means: "*By Which One*

deliberately chooses or decides upon a course of action; a deliberate decision or conclusion; choice. "**Will**" is to do what one chooses, to have one's way and to see fit to one's own thinking.

48

THE DEVIL IS LUST, LIES, AND DELUSIONS; AND
THE MOST IS LOVE AND TRUTH WITHOUT CONFUSION!

CHILDREN OF THE MOST HIGH:
PRISTINE YOUTH AND FAMILY SOLUTIONS, LLC.
SONS AND DAUGHTERS OF THE MOST HIGH PUBLISHERS ®

OH, GRACIOUS MOST HIGH HEAVENLY FATHER, HOLY IS YOUR
NAME, YOUR WILL BE DONE NOW AND FOREVER!

However, in order to sustain staying on the path to the Most High Heavenly Father over time, it is imperative that the children of the Most High only focus on doing the "**Will**" of the Most High Heavenly Father, and to stay focus on doing the works that are in alignment with the "**Will**" of the Most High Heavenly Father's "**Will**" only, now and forever!

In KJV bible book of Matthew chapter 19 verse 26; Yashu'a (Jesus) said: "With men this is impossible; but with God all things are possible." God gave many members of humanity the gift of the ability to think, which **behooves** us to not misuse it and equally, **behooves** us to not under use the gift of the ability to think! One of the most powerful forces in the universe is: "**Thought**" because **thought** initiates all actions **which is maximized through divine love** for the Most High Heavenly Father, **true-prayer supplication** and **true-faith in the Most High**.

THE DEVIL IS LUST, LIES, AND DELUSIONS; AND THE MOST IS LOVE AND TRUTH WITHOUT CONFUSION!

CHILDREN OF THE MOST HIGH:
PRISTINE YOUTH AND FAMILY SOLUTIONS, LLC.
SONS AND DAUGHTERS OF THE MOST HIGH PUBLISHERS ®

OH, GRACIOUS MOST HIGH HEAVENLY FATHER, HOLY IS YOUR NAME, YOUR WILL BE DONE NOW AND FOREVER!

The highest level of knowledge throughout the boundless universes is: **"LOVE"** and **the Most High Heavenly Father is "LOVE".** In KJV bible book of Matthew chapter 22 verses 37-38; Yashu'a (Jesus) said: "Thou shalt love the Lord thy God with all thy heart, and with all thy soul, and with all thy mind. This is the first and great commandment".

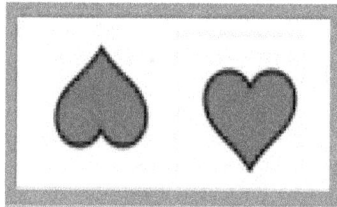

In KJV bible book of Matthew chapter 10 verses 30-40; Yashu'a (Jesus) said: "But the very hairs of your head are all numbered. Fear ye not therefore, ye are of more value than many sparrows. Whosoever therefore shall confess me before men, him will I confess also before my Father which is in heaven."

50

CHILDREN OF THE MOST HIGH:
PRISTINE YOUTH AND FAMILY SOLUTIONS, LLC.
SONS AND DAUGHTERS OF THE MOST HIGH PUBLISHERS ®

OH, GRACIOUS MOST HIGH HEAVENLY FATHER, HOLY IS YOUR
NAME, YOUR WILL BE DONE NOW AND FOREVER!

"But whosoever shall deny me before men, him will I also deny before my Father which is in heaven. <u>Think not that I am come to send peace on earth: I came not to send peace, but a sword.</u> For I am come to set a man at variance against his father, and the daughter against her mother, and the daughter in law against her mother in law. And a man's foes shall be they of his own household. He that loveth father or mother more than me is not worthy of me: and he that loveth son or daughter more than me is not worthy of me. And he that taketh not his cross, and followeth after me, is not worthy of me. He that findeth his life shall lose it: and he that loseth his life for my sake shall find it. He that receiveth you receiveth me, and he that receiveth me receiveth him that sent me."

51

THE DEVIL IS LUST, LIES, AND DELUSIONS; AND
THE MOST IS LOVE AND TRUTH WITHOUT CONFUSION!

CHILDREN OF THE MOST HIGH:
PRISTINE YOUTH AND FAMILY SOLUTIONS, LLC.
SONS AND DAUGHTERS OF THE MOST HIGH PUBLISHERS

OH, GRACIOUS MOST HIGH HEAVENLY FATHER, HOLY IS YOUR
NAME, YOUR WILL BE DONE NOW AND FOREVER!

NATIONAL
SUICIDE
PREVENTION
LIFELINE™
1-800-273-TALK (8255)
suicidepreventionlifeline.org

THE DEVIL IS LUST, LIES, AND DELUSIONS; AND THE MOST IS LOVE AND TRUTH WITHOUT CONFUSION!

CHILDREN OF THE MOST HIGH:
PRISTINE YOUTH AND FAMILY SOLUTIONS, LLC.
SONS AND DAUGHTERS OF THE MOST HIGH PUBLISHERS ®

OH, GRACIOUS MOST HIGH HEAVENLY FATHER, HOLY IS YOUR NAME, YOUR WILL BE DONE NOW AND FOREVER!

53

CHILDREN OF THE MOST HIGH:
PRISTINE YOUTH AND FAMILY SOLUTIONS, LLC.
SONS AND DAUGHTERS OF THE MOST HIGH PUBLISHERS ®

OH, GRACIOUS MOST HIGH HEAVENLY FATHER, HOLY IS YOUR
NAME, YOUR WILL BE DONE NOW AND FOREVER!

In the KJV bible book of 1st John chapter 4 verses 7-10, it states:
"Beloved, let us love one another: for love is of God; and every
one that loveth is born of God, and knoweth God. He that loveth
not knoweth not God; **for God is love**. In this was manifested
the love of God toward us, **because that God sent his only
begotten Son into the world, that we might live through him**.
Herein is love, not that we loved God, but that he loved us, and
sent his Son to be the propitiation for our sins." In the
aforementioned verse, the word: "**Love**" is the KJV bible Greek
Strong's Concordance "**#26** word "ἀγάπη *agape*. **Agape
(Agápē, ag-ah'-pay; ἀγάπη**) means love, i.e. affection or
benevolence; specially (plural) a love-feast: (feast of) charity (-
ably), dear, love." **God is Love and is "The Loving" the devil
is sin, hate, and the hateful!**

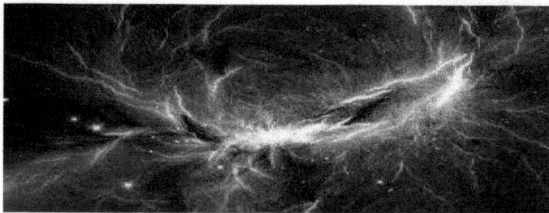

54

CHILDREN OF THE MOST HIGH:
PRISTINE YOUTH AND FAMILY SOLUTIONS, LLC.
SONS AND DAUGHTERS OF THE MOST HIGH PUBLISHERS ®

OH, GRACIOUS MOST HIGH HEAVENLY FATHER, HOLY IS YOUR
NAME, YOUR WILL BE DONE NOW AND FOREVER!

In KJV bible book of Matthew chapter 13 verses 34-35; Yashu'a (Jesus) said: "A new commandment I give unto you, that ye love one another; as I have loved you, that ye also love one another. By this shall all *men* know that ye are my disciples, if ye have love one to another."

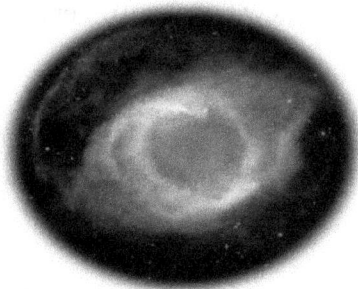

What are the True Vine (Yashu'a, Jesus) other forms of love: 1). Divine Love for the Most High Heavenly Father only. 2). Love of the Messiah Yashu'a (Jesus). 3). Love of parents. 4). Love of siblings. 5). Love of biological children. 6). Love of mate. 7). Love of oneself/one's word. 8). Love of wealth. 9). Love of life. 10). Love of the Prophets. 11). Love of success. 12). Love of fame.

CHILDREN OF THE MOST HIGH:
PRISTINE YOUTH AND FAMILY SOLUTIONS, LLC.
SONS AND DAUGHTERS OF THE MOST HIGH PUBLISHERS ®

What did Yashu'a (Jesus) say is the greatest commandment? In KJV bible book of Matthew chapter 22 verses 37-38; Yashu'a (Jesus) said: "Thou shalt love the Lord thy God with all thy heart, and with all thy soul, and with all thy mind. This is the first and great commandment." In KJV bible book of Matthew chapter 10 verses 30-40; Yashu'a (Jesus) said: "But the very hairs of your head are all numbered. Fear ye not therefore, ye are of more value than many sparrows. Whosoever therefore shall confess me before men, him will I confess also before my Father which is in heaven. But whosoever shall deny me before men, him will I also deny before my Father which is in heaven. Think not that I am come to send peace on earth: I came not to send peace, but a sword. For I am come to set a man at variance against his father, and the daughter against her mother, and the daughter in law against her mother in law. And a man's foes shall be they of his own household."

56

THE DEVIL IS LUST, LIES, AND DELUSIONS; AND THE MOST IS LOVE AND TRUTH WITHOUT CONFUSION!

CHILDREN OF THE MOST HIGH:
PRISTINE YOUTH AND FAMILY SOLUTIONS, LLC.
SONS AND DAUGHTERS OF THE MOST HIGH PUBLISHERS ®

OH, GRACIOUS MOST HIGH HEAVENLY FATHER, HOLY IS YOUR NAME, YOUR WILL BE DONE NOW AND FOREVER!

He that loveth father or mother more than me is not worthy of me: and he that loveth son or daughter more than me is not worthy of me. And he that taketh not his cross, and followeth after me, is not worthy of me. He that findeth his life shall lose it: and he that loseth his life for my sake shall find it. He that receiveth you receiveth me, and he that receiveth me receiveth him that sent me." Therefore, only in obeying this first and great commandment of loving the Lord thy God with all thy heart, and with all thy soul, and with all thy mind, loving the Messiah Yashu'a **(Jesus)** more than our mothers, fathers and children, taking our cross and following the Messiah Yashu'a **(Jesus);** and living our lives in accordance with the example of how the Messiah Yashu'a (Jesus) lived his life, and by **receiving** or accepting the Messiah Yashu'a (Jesus) as our Savior can we be saved and delivered from the lusts, lies and delusions of the devil!

CHILDREN OF THE MOST HIGH:
PRISTINE YOUTH AND FAMILY SOLUTIONS, LLC.
SONS AND DAUGHTERS OF THE MOST HIGH PUBLISHERS ®

OH, GRACIOUS MOST HIGH HEAVENLY FATHER, HOLY IS YOUR
NAME, YOUR WILL BE DONE NOW AND FOREVER!

The **KJV bible Strong's Concordance#1209** is the word "receiveth" is: δέχομαι déchomai, dekh'-om-ahee; middle voice of a primary verb; to receive (in various applications, literally or figuratively): **accep**t, **receive**, take; Yashu'a (Jesus) said: "he that receiveth me receiveth him that sent me." Only by doing so, can a person have a **kingdom of God** in them, **glorifying the Most High as love and truth without confusion** as opposed to a person who has a **kingdom of the devil** in them being deceived by **the devil's lust, lies of the delusions**. **Do you have a kingdom of God moving in you? Or do you have a kingdom of the devil moving in you?**

The aforementioned is for the **children of the Most High** to beware of and to put into moment to moment action to best be able to prevent being deceived by the devil's lust, lies and delusions while simultaneously being empowered, inspired, and guided from moment to moment by the Most High's love and truth without confusion!

58

CHILDREN OF THE MOST HIGH:
PRISTINE YOUTH AND FAMILY SOLUTIONS, LLC.
SONS AND DAUGHTERS OF THE MOST HIGH PUBLISHERS ®

OH, GRACIOUS MOST HIGH HEAVENLY FATHER, HOLY IS YOUR
NAME, YOUR WILL BE DONE NOW AND FOREVER!

**Chapter 2: Mirror, Mirror on the Wall; Oh, Most High;
Help us to become the best that we can Become in All!**

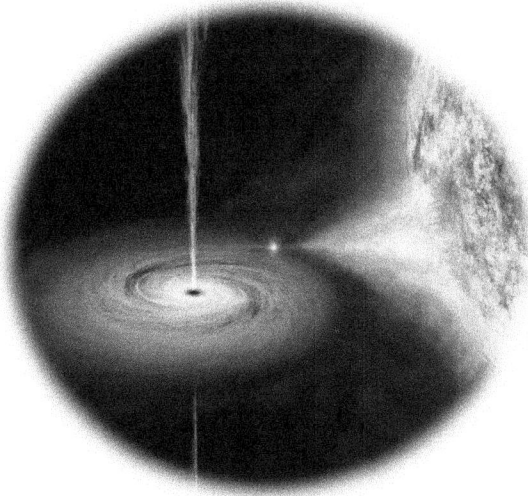

*"Create in me a clean heart,
O God; and renew a right spirit within me, KJV
bible book of Psalms, chapter 51 verse 10."*

CHILDREN OF THE MOST HIGH:
PRISTINE YOUTH AND FAMILY SOLUTIONS, LLC.
SONS AND DAUGHTERS OF THE MOST HIGH PUBLISHERS ®

OH, GRACIOUS MOST HIGH HEAVENLY FATHER, HOLY IS YOUR
NAME, YOUR WILL BE DONE NOW AND FOREVER!

When you look in the mirror, or when you see a picture of yourself, do you predominately see a **peacemaker**? Or a **troublemaker**? Does the person that you see in the mirror have a heart that is ruled by lust and love of the world? Or does the person that you see in the mirror have a heart that is ruled by the love of God?

CHILDREN OF THE MOST HIGH:
PRISTINE YOUTH AND FAMILY SOLUTIONS, LLC.
SONS AND DAUGHTERS OF THE MOST HIGH PUBLISHERS ®

OH, GRACIOUS MOST HIGH HEAVENLY FATHER, HOLY IS YOUR
NAME, YOUR WILL BE DONE NOW AND FOREVER!

In the KJV bible book of 2nd Timothy chapter 3 verses 1-5; it states: "**In the last days perilous times shall come. For [people]** (ἄνθρωπος anthrōpos – male and female human beings) **shall be lovers of their own selves**, covetous, boasters, proud, blasphemers, disobedient to parents, unthankful, unholy, without natural affection, trucebreakers, false accusers, incontinent, fierce, despisers of those that are good, traitors, heady, high-minded, lovers of pleasures more than lovers of God. Having a form of godliness, but denying the power thereof: from such turn away." In the KJV bible book of Matthew chapter 6 verse 33; the Messiah Yashu'a (Jesus) said: "But seek ye first the kingdom of God, and his righteousness; and all these things shall be added unto you."

CHILDREN OF THE MOST HIGH:
PRISTINE YOUTH AND FAMILY SOLUTIONS, LLC.
SONS AND DAUGHTERS OF THE MOST HIGH PUBLISHERS ®

OH, GRACIOUS MOST HIGH HEAVENLY FATHER, HOLY IS YOUR
NAME, YOUR WILL BE DONE NOW AND FOREVER!

In the KJV of the bible chapter of 1st John chapter 2 verse 15; it states: "**Love not the world, neither the things that are in the world**. If any **man** (**the original Greek word in this verse for "man" is τὶς tìs, and literally means any person regardless of gender**) love the world, the love of the Father is not in him [**or her**]." When you look in the mirror, or when you see a picture of yourself, what is **the content of the character** of the reflection that you see?

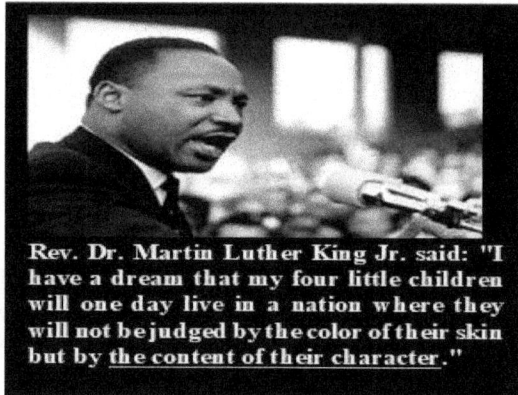

Rev. Dr. Martin Luther King Jr. said: "I have a dream that my four little children will one day live in a nation where they will not be judged by the color of their skin but by the content of their character."

62

CHILDREN OF THE MOST HIGH:
PRISTINE YOUTH AND FAMILY SOLUTIONS, LLC.
SONS AND DAUGHTERS OF THE MOST HIGH PUBLISHERS ®

What do the words: **content** and **character** mean? According to the Online Merriam Webster Dictionary (2020), the word "**content**" is defined as: "**something contained; principle substance**, and **complex parts**." The word "**character**" is defined as: "**the complex of mental and ethical traits marking and often individualizing a person,** group, or nation; **main or essential nature** especially as strongly marked and serving to distinguish." When you look in the mirror, or when you see a picture of yourself; what is the **nature** of the being that you see? Do you have the **nature** of the **children of the devil**? Or do you have the **nature** of the **children of the Most High** (God)? In the KJV bible, **other than a physical human father**; there are only **2 fathers** spoken of in the KJV bible. The **only 2 fathers** spoken of in the KJV bible are the **devil** and the **Most High** (God).

63

THE DEVIL IS LUST, LIES, AND DELUSIONS; AND THE MOST IS LOVE AND TRUTH WITHOUT CONFUSION!

CHILDREN OF THE MOST HIGH:
PRISTINE YOUTH AND FAMILY SOLUTIONS, LLC.
SONS AND DAUGHTERS OF THE MOST HIGH PUBLISHERS ®

OH, GRACIOUS MOST HIGH HEAVENLY FATHER, HOLY IS YOUR NAME, YOUR WILL BE DONE NOW AND FOREVER!

In the KJV bible book of John chapter 8 verse 44, Yashu'a (Jesus) said: "Ye are of <u>your father the devil</u>, and the lusts of your father ye will do. He was a murderer from the beginning, and abode not in the truth, because there is "No truth in him. When he speaketh a lie, he speaketh of his own: for he is a liar, and the father of it." In the KJV bible book of Matthew chapter 5 verse 9; Yashu'a (Jesus) said: "Blessed <u>are the peacemakers</u>: for they shall be <u>called the children of God</u>." The word "εἰρηνοποιός **eirēnopoios**" for the words: "**<u>are the peacemakers</u>**" in the KJV bible Greek Strong's Concordance is "**#1518 word "eirēnopoios"** pronounced as: **ā-rā-no-poi-o's** and means "**a peacemaker; pacific, loving peace**." In the KJV bible book of 1st John chapter 3 verses 9-10; it states: "Whosoever is born of God doeth not commit sin; for his **seed** remained in him: and he cannot sin, because he is born of God. In this **<u>the children of God</u>** are manifest, and **<u>the children of the devil:</u>** whosoever doeth not righteousness is not of God, neither he that loveth not his brother."

64

CHILDREN OF THE MOST HIGH:
PRISTINE YOUTH AND FAMILY SOLUTIONS, LLC.
SONS AND DAUGHTERS OF THE MOST HIGH PUBLISHERS ®

OH, GRACIOUS MOST HIGH HEAVENLY FATHER, HOLY IS YOUR
NAME, YOUR WILL BE DONE NOW AND FOREVER!

In the eyesight of the Most High Heavenly Father, do you think
that you are at your best when you are obeying the Most High
commandments? Or do you think that you are at your best when
you are disobeying the Most High commandments?

In the KJV bible book of Exodus chapter 20 verse 4 states:
"Thou shall not bare **false witness** against thy neighbour," what
does the words "**false witness**" mean? According the KJV bible
Hebrew Strong's Concordance "#867, the word for: "**false**" is
שֶׁקֶר **sheqer pronounced as: sheh'·ker**, and **means:** "deception
(what deceives or disappoints or betrays one); deceit, fraud,
wrong; fraudulently, wrongfully (as adverb); falsehood
(injurious in testimony); testify falsehood, false oath, swear
falsely; falsity (of false or self-deceived prophets); lie,
falsehood (in general); false tongue; in vain." According the
KJV bible Hebrew Strong's Concordance#5707, the word for:
"**witness**" is עֵד `**ed pronounced as: ād** and means: "witness,
testimony, evidence (of things); witness (of people)."

65

THE DEVIL IS LUST, LIES, AND DELUSIONS; AND
THE MOST IS LOVE AND TRUTH WITHOUT CONFUSION!

CHILDREN OF THE MOST HIGH:
PRISTINE YOUTH AND FAMILY SOLUTIONS, LLC.
SONS AND DAUGHTERS OF THE MOST HIGH PUBLISHERS ®

OH, GRACIOUS MOST HIGH HEAVENLY FATHER, HOLY IS YOUR
NAME, YOUR WILL BE DONE NOW AND FOREVER!

So, a "**false witness**" is **a witness that lies by giving an untrue testimony**. Are you on social media? Have you ever seen someone who is a social media **false witness**? **If so, does your social media posts/messages reflect lust, lies, and delusion; vanity and/or the love of money**?

Or **do your social media posts/messages reflect that the Most High Heavenly Father is love and truth without confusion**? If you **are or are not** on social media, how much time in a day does your mind think about **lust, lies, and delusion; vanity and/or the love of money**? If you **are or are not** on social media, how much time in a day does your heart desire **lust, lies, and delusion; vanity and/or the love of money**? If you **are or are not** on social media, how much time in a day does your mind think thoughts that reflect that the **Most High is love and truth without confusion**?

THE DEVIL IS LUST, LIES, AND DELUSIONS; AND
THE MOST IS LOVE AND TRUTH WITHOUT CONFUSION!

CHILDREN OF THE MOST HIGH:
PRISTINE YOUTH AND FAMILY SOLUTIONS, LLC.
SONS AND DAUGHTERS OF THE MOST HIGH PUBLISHERS ®

OH, GRACIOUS MOST HIGH HEAVENLY FATHER, HOLY IS YOUR
NAME, YOUR WILL BE DONE NOW AND FOREVER!

If you **are or are not** on social media, how much time in a day does your heart desire to be a recipient of the **Most High Heavenly Father's love and truth without confusion**?

In the KJV bible book of 2nd Thessalonians chapter 2 verse 11 states: "And for this cause, God shall send them strong **delusion**, that **they should believe a lie**." In the KJV bible Greek Strong's Concordance#**4106**, the word for: "**delusion**" is πλάνη **plane**, and means: "**one led astray from the right way, roams hither and thither; mental straying; error, wrong opinion relative to morals or religion; error which shows itself in action, a wrong mode of acting; that which leads into error, deceit or fraud**."

67

CHILDREN OF THE MOST HIGH:
PRISTINE YOUTH AND FAMILY SOLUTIONS, LLC.
SONS AND DAUGHTERS OF THE MOST HIGH PUBLISHERS ®

OH, GRACIOUS MOST HIGH HEAVENLY FATHER, HOLY IS YOUR
NAME, YOUR WILL BE DONE NOW AND FOREVER!

What is delusion of grandeur? According to the Online Mayo Clinic Website (2020), **a delusion of grandeur** is the <u>**false belief**</u> in one's own superiority, greatness, or intelligence. People experiencing **delusions of grandeur** do not just have high self-esteem; instead, they believe in their own greatness and importance <u>**even in the face of overwhelming evidence to the contrary**</u>. According to the Online Merriam-Webster Dictionary (2020), **Delusion of grandeur** is defined as: **"something that is falsely or delusively believed or propagated**. A **delusion** is a belief that is clearly false and that indicates an abnormality in the affected person's content of thought. The false belief is not accounted for by the person's cultural or religious background or his or her level of intelligence. The key feature of a delusion is the degree to which the person is convinced that the belief is true. A person with a delusion will hold firmly to the belief regardless of evidence to the contrary."

CHILDREN OF THE MOST HIGH:
PRISTINE YOUTH AND FAMILY SOLUTIONS, LLC.
SONS AND DAUGHTERS OF THE MOST HIGH PUBLISHERS ®

OH, GRACIOUS MOST HIGH HEAVENLY FATHER, HOLY IS YOUR
NAME, YOUR WILL BE DONE NOW AND FOREVER!

"**Delusions of grandeur** can be difficult to distinguish from overvalued ideas, which are unreasonable ideas that a person holds, but the affected person has at least some level of doubt as to its truthfulness. A person with a **delusion** is absolutely convinced that the **delusion** is real. **Delusions of grandeur** are a symptom of either a medical, neurological, or mental disorder." "**Delusions of grandeur** may be present in any of the following mental disorders: (1) Psychotic disorders, or disorders in which the affected person has a diminished or distorted sense of reality and cannot distinguish the real from the unreal, including schizophrenia, schizoaffective disorder, delusional disorder, schizophreniform disorder, shared psychotic disorder, brief psychotic disorder, and substance-induced psychotic disorder, (2) Bipolar disorder, (3) Major depressive disorder with psychotic features (4) Delirium, and (5) Dementia, (Online Merriam-Webster Dictionary, 2020)."

CHILDREN OF THE MOST HIGH:
PRISTINE YOUTH AND FAMILY SOLUTIONS, LLC.
SONS AND DAUGHTERS OF THE MOST HIGH PUBLISHERS ®

OH, GRACIOUS MOST HIGH HEAVENLY FATHER, HOLY IS YOUR
NAME, YOUR WILL BE DONE NOW AND FOREVER!

In the KJV bible book of James chapter 3 verse 16-18, it states: "For where **envying** and **strife** *is*, there *is* **confusion** and **every evil work**. But the wisdom that is from above is first pure, then peaceable, gentle, and easy to be intreated, full of mercy and good fruits, without partiality, and without hypocrisy. **And the fruit of righteousness is sown in peace of them that make peace**." In the KJV bible Greek Strong's Concordance#**4106**, the word for: "**is confusion**" is ἀκαταστασία akatastasia, pronounced: **ä-kä-tä-stä-sē'-ä**; and is defined as: "**instability, a state of disorder, disturbance, confusion**."

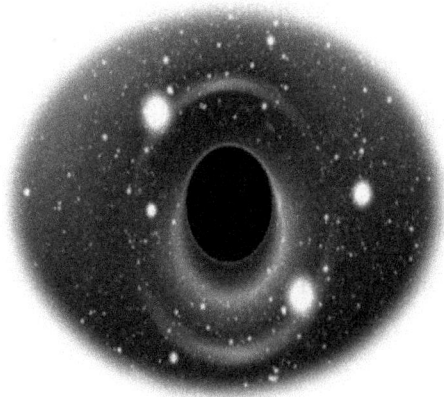

70

THE DEVIL IS LUST, LIES, AND DELUSIONS; AND
THE MOST IS LOVE AND TRUTH WITHOUT CONFUSION!

CHILDREN OF THE MOST HIGH:
PRISTINE YOUTH AND FAMILY SOLUTIONS, LLC.
SONS AND DAUGHTERS OF THE MOST HIGH PUBLISHERS ®

OH, GRACIOUS MOST HIGH HEAVENLY FATHER, HOLY IS YOUR
NAME, YOUR WILL BE DONE NOW AND FOREVER!

What do the words: delusion, confusion, lie, **liar**, and **lying**, mean? According to the Online Merriam Webster Dictionary (2020), the word "**delusion**" is defined as: "something that is falsely or delusively believed or propagated under the delusion that they will finish on schedule delusions of grandeur; a persistent false psychotic belief regarding the self or persons or objects outside the self that is maintained despite indisputable evidence to the contrary; and the act of tricking or deceiving someone; the state of being deluded." The word "**confusion**" is defined as: "an act or instance of confusing; confusion of the issue; the quality or state of being confused; mental confusion; a confused mass or mixture; a confusion of voices." The word "**lie**" is defined as: "to make an untrue statement with intent to deceive: to create a false or misleading impression. to bring about by telling lies; an assertion of something known or believed by the speaker or writer to be untrue with intent to deceive; an untrue or inaccurate statement; something that misleads or deceives."

71

CHILDREN OF THE MOST HIGH:
PRISTINE YOUTH AND FAMILY SOLUTIONS, LLC.
SONS AND DAUGHTERS OF THE MOST HIGH PUBLISHERS ®

OH, GRACIOUS MOST HIGH HEAVENLY FATHER, HOLY IS YOUR
NAME, YOUR WILL BE DONE NOW AND FOREVER!

The word "**liar**" is defined as: "a person who tells lies." The word "**lying**" is defined as: "dishonest, mendacious, untruthful according to the Online Merriam Webster Dictionary (2020)." Is the person that you see when you look into a mirror reflecting **a lying child of the devil**? Or **a truthful child of the Most High (God)**? Does being one of the children of the devil or children of the Most High, matter to you? If so, why? If not, why not?

According to the bible, are there benefits to being a person who tells the truth? In the KJV bible book of Revelation chapter 22 verses 14-16; Yashu'a (Jesus) saith "Blessed are they that do his commandments, that they may have right to the tree of life, and may enter in through the gates into the city."

THE DEVIL IS LUST, LIES, AND DELUSIONS; AND
THE MOST IS LOVE AND TRUTH WITHOUT CONFUSION!

CHILDREN OF THE MOST HIGH:
PRISTINE YOUTH AND FAMILY SOLUTIONS, LLC.
SONS AND DAUGHTERS OF THE MOST HIGH PUBLISHERS ®

OH, GRACIOUS MOST HIGH HEAVENLY FATHER, HOLY IS YOUR
NAME, YOUR WILL BE DONE NOW AND FOREVER!

CHILDREN OF THE MOST HIGH:
PRISTINE YOUTH AND FAMILY SOLUTIONS, LLC.
SONS AND DAUGHTERS OF THE MOST HIGH PUBLISHERS ®

THE DEVIL'S WEB

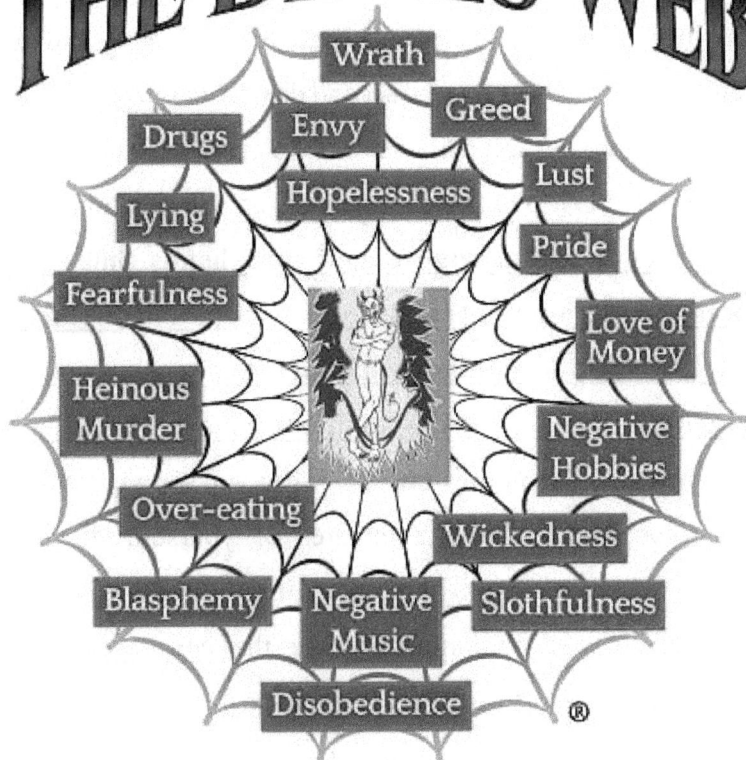

Wrath

Greed

Drugs

Envy

Hopelessness

Lust

Lying

Pride

Fearfulness

Love of
Money

Heinous
Murder

Negative
Hobbies

Over-eating

Wickedness

Blasphemy

Negative
Music

Slothfulness

Disobedience ®

73

CHILDREN OF THE MOST HIGH:
PRISTINE YOUTH AND FAMILY SOLUTIONS, LLC.
SONS AND DAUGHTERS OF THE MOST HIGH PUBLISHERS ®

OH, GRACIOUS MOST HIGH HEAVENLY FATHER, HOLY IS YOUR
NAME, YOUR WILL BE DONE NOW AND FOREVER!

According to the bible, are there consequences for liars?
Yes! In the KJV bible book of Revelation, chapter 21 verse 8; it states: "But the fearful, and unbelieving, and the abominable, and murderers, and whoremongers, and sorcerers, and idolaters, and all **liars**, shall have their part in the lake which burneth with fire and brimstone: which is the second death." In the KJV bible book of Proverbs chapter 6 verses 16-19 it states: "These six things doth the LORD hate: yea, seven are an abomination unto him: **A proud look**, **a lying tongue**, **and hands that shed innocent blood**, **a heart that deviseth wicked imaginations**, **feet that be swift in running to mischief**, **A false witness that speaketh lies**, and **he that soweth discord among brethren**." Now, when you look in the mirror, or when you see a picture of yourself, or when you take pictures of yourself, do you predominately see the **content of the character children of the devil**? Or do you predominately see the **content of the character children of the Most High (God)**?

74

CHILDREN OF THE MOST HIGH:
PRISTINE YOUTH AND FAMILY SOLUTIONS, LLC.
SONS AND DAUGHTERS OF THE MOST HIGH PUBLISHERS ®

OH, GRACIOUS MOST HIGH HEAVENLY FATHER, HOLY IS YOUR
NAME, YOUR WILL BE DONE NOW AND FOREVER!

The truthful answers to these questions are essential for those who don't want to be deceived by the devil's lusts, lies and delusions; but rather acknowledge that the Most High is love and truth without confusion!

The aforementioned is for the children of the Most High to beware of and to put into moment to moment practice to best be able to prevent being deceived by the devil's lust, lies and delusions while simultaneously being empowered, inspired, and guided from moment to moment by the Most High's love and truth without confusion!

CHILDREN OF THE MOST HIGH:
PRISTINE YOUTH AND FAMILY SOLUTIONS, LLC.
SONS AND DAUGHTERS OF THE MOST HIGH PUBLISHERS ®

OH, GRACIOUS MOST HIGH HEAVENLY FATHER, HOLY IS YOUR
NAME, YOUR WILL BE DONE NOW AND FOREVER!

Chapter 3: God is Love and Truth and the Devil is Lust and Lies!

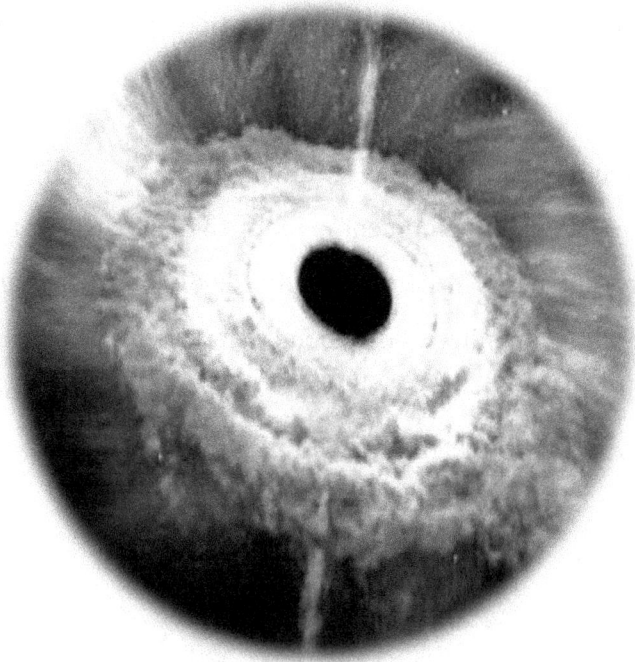

In the KJV bible book of Jeremiah chapter 29 verse 13; it states: "And ye shall seek me, and find me, when ye shall search for me with all your heart."

CHILDREN OF THE MOST HIGH:
PRISTINE YOUTH AND FAMILY SOLUTIONS, LLC.
SONS AND DAUGHTERS OF THE MOST HIGH PUBLISHERS ®

In the KJV bible book of Genesis Chapter 1 verse 1; is God singular or plural?

The KJV bible book of Genesis Chapter 1 verse 1 with modern Hebrew inserts, states: 1:1 בְּרֵאשִׁית בָּרָא אֱלֹהִים אֵת הַשָּׁמַיִם וְאֵת הָאָרֶץ: In the **beginning רֵאשִׁית Re'Shiyth** God **(KJV bible Hebrew Strong's Concordance#430) אֱלֹהִים 'Elohiym created בָּרָא Bara'** (Khalaq) the heaven **שָׁמַיִם Shamayim** and **אֵת 'eth** the earth **אֶרֶץ 'Erets**. In the KJV bible book of Genesis Chapter 1 verse 1, the **original Aramic/Hebrew plural word "Elohiym"** was translated into the **English singular word: "God"**. According to the "King James Bible Hebrew Strong's Concordance: "#430 "Elohiym" (God)** is the **original Aramic/Hebrew word: אֱלֹהִים "Elohiym"** Phonetic Spelling: **(El-o-heem')**, is a **Plural** word that means: (1), **Gods** (204), great (2), **judges** (3), mighty (2), **rulers** (1), shrine* (1). **plural in number**. a. rulers, judges, either as divine representatives at sacred places or as reflecting divine majesty and power: b. **divine ones, superhuman beings.**"

77

CHILDREN OF THE MOST HIGH:
PRISTINE YOUTH AND FAMILY SOLUTIONS, LLC.
SONS AND DAUGHTERS OF THE MOST HIGH PUBLISHERS ®

OH, GRACIOUS MOST HIGH HEAVENLY FATHER, HOLY IS YOUR NAME, YOUR WILL BE DONE NOW AND FOREVER!

As the aforementioned reflects, **the correct translation** of Genesis Chapter 1 verse 1 **would be**: In the beginning, the **Gods** created the heavens and the earth. **Those** or **these beings**; "**Gods**" **are part of the Most High Heavenly Father's Guardian-Angelic Hosts**. It is one of the Children of the Most High: Pristine Youth and Family Solutions, LLC. greatest hopes that members of humanity will now be aware that by studying the scriptures in the languages that they were revealed in, can empower the sincere-hearted person by them being able to receive the original messages in the scriptures that he or she was intended to receive. In KJV bible book of Psalms chapter 82 verse 1 with Hebrew inserts, it states: "**82:1 מִזְמוֹר לְאָסָף** אֱלֹהִים נִצָּב בַּעֲדַת־אֵל בְּקֶרֶב אֱלֹהִים יִשְׁפֹּט׃ **God** (KJV bible Hebrew Strong's Concordance#**430 אֱלֹהִים 'Elohiym, plural**) standeth in the congregation עֵדָה `edah of the mighty אֵל 'el he judgeth שָׁפַט shaphat among קֶרֶב qereb the gods (KJV bible Hebrew Strong's Concordance#**430 אֱלֹהִים** 'Elohiym, plural).

78

THE DEVIL IS LUST, LIES, AND DELUSIONS; AND
THE MOST IS LOVE AND TRUTH WITHOUT CONFUSION!

CHILDREN OF THE MOST HIGH:
PRISTINE YOUTH AND FAMILY SOLUTIONS, LLC.
SONS AND DAUGHTERS OF THE MOST HIGH PUBLISHERS ®

OH, GRACIOUS MOST HIGH HEAVENLY FATHER, HOLY IS YOUR
NAME, YOUR WILL BE DONE NOW AND FOREVER!

In the previous KJV bible book of Psalms chapter 82 verse 1, the Aramic/Hebrew word for "God" and "gods" is the same Aramic/Hebrew word: "**Elohiym אֱלֹהִים**" it states: "**God**" standeth in the congregation of the mighty; he judgeth among the "**gods**" (being that the words "**God**" and "**gods**" in this verse **is translated from the exact same original Aramic/Hebrew word**: "Elohiym אֱלֹהִים"; which is a plural. **The truth is that there are no lower-case letters in the Hebrew language, so everywhere you see a small "g"; it is incorrect and may lead the sincere-hearted truth seeker astray**. The Greek equivalent to the Aramic/Hebrew "Elohiym" (Gods) is **Theos** (God) as used in KJV bible book of John chapter 10 verse 34. **Also, there are no lower-case letters in the Greek language, so everywhere you see a small "g"; it is incorrect and may lead the sincere-hearted truth seeker astray**. **Why does this matter**? This matters' if you don't want to be deceived by the devil's delusions which are the root causes of intentional **real lies (realized)** misinterpretations of the original languages that the bible was revealed in.

79

THE DEVIL IS LUST, LIES, AND DELUSIONS; AND
THE MOST IS LOVE AND TRUTH WITHOUT CONFUSION!

CHILDREN OF THE MOST HIGH:
PRISTINE YOUTH AND FAMILY SOLUTIONS, LLC.
SONS AND DAUGHTERS OF THE MOST HIGH PUBLISHERS ®

OH, GRACIOUS MOST HIGH HEAVENLY FATHER, HOLY IS YOUR
NAME, YOUR WILL BE DONE NOW AND FOREVER!

This also matters to sincere-hearted people who only want to learn the non-bias original messages that are in the original language that the bible was revealed in. This is necessary, in an effort to acquire the original messages that the **Elohiym (God)** intended on us receiving before the original biblical scriptures were translated hundreds or more times, differently than in the original languages they were revealed in. This also matters to the real followers of **Yashu'a Ha Mashiakh (Jesus the Messiah)** because he said in the KJV bible book of John chapter 8 verse 32: "And ye shall know the truth, and the truth shall make you free." "Ye shall know" (γινώσκω **ginōskō,** is KJV bible Greek Strong's Concordance#1097 word: γινώσκω **ginōskō,** which means **to know, understand, perceive**). The word **"translation"** means the act or process of translating, especially from one language into another.

80

THE DEVIL IS LUST, LIES, AND DELUSIONS; AND
THE MOST IS LOVE AND TRUTH WITHOUT CONFUSION!

CHILDREN OF THE MOST HIGH:
PRISTINE YOUTH AND FAMILY SOLUTIONS, LLC.
SONS AND DAUGHTERS OF THE MOST HIGH PUBLISHERS ℗

OH, GRACIOUS MOST HIGH HEAVENLY FATHER, HOLY IS YOUR
NAME, YOUR WILL BE DONE NOW AND FOREVER!

So, in order to ensure that sincere-hearted people who have accepted the real Messiah Yashu'a (Jesus) as their Savior are **not being _deceived_** by modern day mistranslations of the bible; and to ensure that they **know the truth**; we must make the time to do intense, evidence-based, non-bias, rigorous research into the original languages that the bible and other scriptures were revealed in. In other words, sincere-hearted people who have accepted the real Messiah Yashu'a (Jesus) as their Savior have to study the bible from a **Messiah con_scio_usness and Spirit of the Messiah Yashu'a** (Jesus) **_scien_**ce of the seen and unseen perspective in order **to know the truth that will make you free**. According to the Online American Heritage Dictionary (2020), science is defined as: **sci·ence** - (sī`əns) [From Middle English, knowledge, learning, from Old French, from Latin _scientia_, from _sciēn_, _scient-_, present participle of _scīre_, **to know**; from the root word **scio – to know**;

81

CHILDREN OF THE MOST HIGH:
PRISTINE YOUTH AND FAMILY SOLUTIONS, LLC.
SONS AND DAUGHTERS OF THE MOST HIGH PUBLISHERS ®

OH, GRACIOUS MOST HIGH HEAVENLY FATHER, HOLY IS YOUR
NAME, YOUR WILL BE DONE NOW AND FOREVER!

n.**1.** **a.** The observation, identification, description, experimental investigation, and theoretical explanation of phenomena: *new advances in science and technology.* **b.** Such activities restricted to a class of natural phenomena: *the science of astronomy.* **2.** A systematic method or body of knowledge in a given area: *the science of marketing.* **3.** *Archaic* Knowledge, especially that gained through experience. According to the Latdict, Latin dictionary and grammar resources (2016), **SCIO** is defined as a: verb: **know, understand;** So, according to the aforementioned, sincere-hearted people who have accepted the real Messiah Yashu'a (Jesus) as their Savior have to study the bible from a **Messiah con*scio*usness** and **Spirit of the Messiah Yashu'a** (Jesus) **scie**nce of the seen and unseen perspective in order **to know the truth that will make you free**.

CHILDREN OF THE MOST HIGH:
PRISTINE YOUTH AND FAMILY SOLUTIONS, LLC.
SONS AND DAUGHTERS OF THE MOST HIGH PUBLISHERS ®

OH, GRACIOUS MOST HIGH HEAVENLY FATHER, HOLY IS YOUR
NAME, YOUR WILL BE DONE NOW AND FOREVER!

Now, members of humanity have an opportunity to utilize the Hebrew-Greek Key Word Study King James Version of the Bible and Strong's Concordance to research the bible, word by word in the original languages they were revealed in **via cellphone free apps or online free apps**. This may lead to members of humanity learning and knowing the truth that will make them free just as the Messiah Yashu'a (Jesus) said that it would. This process is essential for those who don't want to be deceived by the devil's lusts, lies and delusions; but rather acknowledge that the Most High is love and truth without confusion! **In relations to Elohiym being the pluralization of the title: "God", according to the bible, <u>who is the Most High</u>? Who** (phonetically is HU), **HU is the Ancient African creative source and creative force of will. The Most High Heavenly Father is Love, the Sustainer, the Nourisher, the Provider of all Life, and the Omnipotent and the Omnipresent Creator of the boundless universes.**

83

CHILDREN OF THE MOST HIGH:
PRISTINE YOUTH AND FAMILY SOLUTIONS, LLC.
SONS AND DAUGHTERS OF THE MOST HIGH PUBLISHERS ®

OH, GRACIOUS MOST HIGH HEAVENLY FATHER, HOLY IS YOUR
NAME, YOUR WILL BE DONE NOW AND FOREVER!

The Most High Heavenly Father encompasses and
interpenetrates all existence inclusive of every part of nature
both visible as well as invisible. The Most High Heavenly
Father eternally extends from within all existence and creation.
**Oh, Most High Heavenly One, you are all, and there is
nothing nearer to us than you; for you encompass all things!**
Glory be to you alone! In the KJV bible book of John chapter 4
verse 23; the Messiah Yashu'a (Jesus) said: "God is a Spirit:
and they that worship him must worship him in spirit and
in truth." In the KJV bible book of Genesis, chapter 14 verse
18; it states: "And Melchizedek (**Malkiy-Tsedeq, מַלְכִּי־צֶדֶק**)
king of Salem (שָׁלֵם **Shalem** or **Shalom** means **Peace**. So,
according to the bible, **Malkiy-Tsedeq, מַלְכִּי־צֶדֶק is the king of
peace**) brought forth bread and wine: and he was the priest of
the Most High (**ELYOWN עֶלְיוֹן EL אֵל**) God." Is Yashu'a
(Jesus) Melchizedek? **No. Yashu'a (Jesus) is after the Order
of Melchizedek**.

84

THE DEVIL IS LUST, LIES, AND DELUSIONS; AND
THE MOST IS LOVE AND TRUTH WITHOUT CONFUSION!

CHILDREN OF THE MOST HIGH:
PRISTINE YOUTH AND FAMILY SOLUTIONS, LLC.
SONS AND DAUGHTERS OF THE MOST HIGH PUBLISHERS ®

OH, GRACIOUS MOST HIGH HEAVENLY FATHER, HOLY IS YOUR
NAME, YOUR WILL BE DONE NOW AND FOREVER!

In the KJV bible book of Hebrews, chapter 5 verses 5-6; it states: "So also, Christ glorified not himself to be made a high priest; but he that said unto him, thou art my Son, today have I begotten thee. As he saith also in another place, **Thou art a priest <u>forever after the order of Melchisedec</u>**."

It is critical that all children of the Most High know the differences between "**God**" ("אֱלֹהִים 'Elohiym") in the KJV bible book of Genesis chapter 1 verse 1, "**The LORD, יְהֹוָה Yĕhovah, (Yahuwa, Yahweh, Jehovah, Yahayyu)**" who repented to **the Most High (ELYOWN עֶלְיוֹן EL אֵל)** in the KJV bible book of Genesis chapter 6 verse 6; "the LORD, and the יְהֹוָה Yĕhovah "**God**" "**אֱלֹהִים 'Elohiym**" who gets jealous in the KJV bible book of Exodus chapter 20 verse 5; **ARE NOT TO BE CONFUSED AS BEING the Most High (ELYOWN עֶלְיוֹן EL אֵל)**, the Sustainer, the Nourisher, the Provider of all Life, and the Omnipotent and the Omnipresent Creator of the boundless universes who they all worship and do the "**Will**" of!

85

CHILDREN OF THE MOST HIGH:
PRISTINE YOUTH AND FAMILY SOLUTIONS, LLC.
SONS AND DAUGHTERS OF THE MOST HIGH PUBLISHERS ®

OH, GRACIOUS MOST HIGH HEAVENLY FATHER, HOLY IS YOUR
NAME, YOUR WILL BE DONE NOW AND FOREVER!

In the KJV bible book of Psalms chapter 82 verse 6; it states: "I have said, Ye are gods; and all of you are children of <u>the Most High</u>. The title: "**Most High**" is: the KJV bible Hebrew Strong's Concordance "**#5945 ELYOWN** עֶלְיוֹן **EL** א for the title: "**Most High**" (ELYOWN עֶלְיוֹן EL **אֵל**), **which means:** "<u>Highest</u>, **Most High**, <u>Name of God</u>, **as title,** <u>The Supreme:</u>—(Most, on) high(-er, -est), upper(-most)." The title: "**God'** <u>in this verse</u> is the KJV bible Hebrew Strong's Concordance **#5945** for the title: "**God**" (**EL** אֵל), **which means: "God, god, power, mighty, goodly, great, idols, might, strong, god, god-like one, mighty one, mighty men, men of rank, mighty heroes, angels, god, false god, (demons, imaginations), and mighty things in nature."** In the KJV bible book of Numbers chapter 23 verse 19; states: "**God (EL אֵל) <u>is not a man, that he should lie; neither the son of man, that he should repent: hath he said, and shall he not do it? or hath he spoken, and shall he not make it good</u>?"**

CHILDREN OF THE MOST HIGH:
PRISTINE YOUTH AND FAMILY SOLUTIONS, LLC.
SONS AND DAUGHTERS OF THE MOST HIGH PUBLISHERS ®

OH, GRACIOUS MOST HIGH HEAVENLY FATHER, HOLY IS YOUR
NAME, YOUR WILL BE DONE NOW AND FOREVER!

The above mentioned KJV bible Hebrew Strong's Concordance original Aramaic/Hebrew words/verses, confirmed and substantiated the **True Vine (Yashu'a, Jesus) realities**. This matters to the real followers of **Yashu'a Ha Mashiakh (Jesus the Messiah)** because he said in the KJV bible book of John chapter 8 verse 32: "And ye shall know the truth, and the truth shall make you free." **"Ye shall know"** (γινώσκω **ginōskō, is Strong's concordance #1097 and means to know, understand, perceive).**

According to the Bible and the Qur'aan/Qur'an or Koran; what are the diversity of titles for the being that is called: "The Devil"? First, it is important that the children of the Most High know that there are many devils or what is referred to as devils. Each exhibiting diverse personalities at different places and spaces of time depending on a plethora of known and unknown variables.

87

CHILDREN OF THE MOST HIGH:
PRISTINE YOUTH AND FAMILY SOLUTIONS, LLC.
SONS AND DAUGHTERS OF THE MOST HIGH PUBLISHERS ®

OH, GRACIOUS MOST HIGH HEAVENLY FATHER, HOLY IS YOUR
NAME, YOUR WILL BE DONE NOW AND FOREVER!

For example, unbeknown to many of us in the body of
Christ, <u>Lucifer has a father and his father</u> is mentioned in
the bible. In the KJV bible book of Isaiah chapter 14 verse 12.
The KJV bible book of Isaiah chapter 14 verse 12 with Hebrew
inserts states: אֵיךְ נָפַלְתָּ מִשָּׁמַיִם הֵילֵל בֶּן־שָׁחַר נִגְדַּעְתָּ לָאָרֶץ חוֹלֵשׁ
עַל־גּוֹיִם: "How art thou fallen (נָפַל Naphal) from heaven (שָׁמַיִם
Shamayim) O <u>Lucifer</u> (הֵילֵל Haylal, Hêylêl, Hay-lale') <u>son</u> (בֶּן
Ben) of **the morning** (שָׁחַר Shakhar (Shachar) (יְלַל Yalal)
how art thou cut down (גָּדַע Gada`) to the ground (אֶרֶץ 'Erets)
which didst weaken (**Chalash**) the nations (גּוֹי Gowy)."

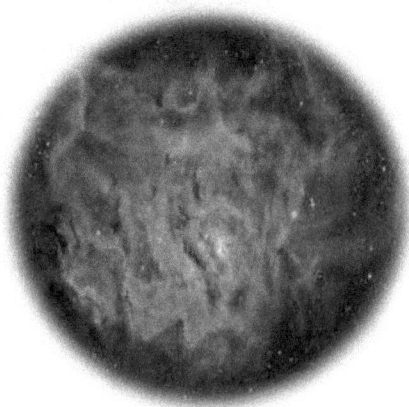

88

CHILDREN OF THE MOST HIGH:
PRISTINE YOUTH AND FAMILY SOLUTIONS, LLC.
SONS AND DAUGHTERS OF THE MOST HIGH PUBLISHERS ®

OH, GRACIOUS MOST HIGH HEAVENLY FATHER, HOLY IS YOUR
NAME, YOUR WILL BE DONE NOW AND FOREVER!

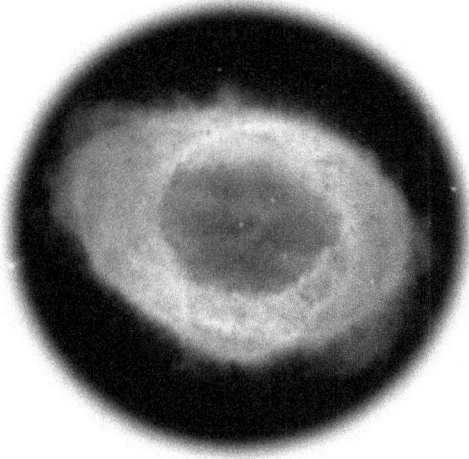

The aforementioned verse in the original Aramic (Hebrew) language makes it very clear that **Lucifer** or **Satan** <u>**is the son of his father**</u> שַׁחַר **Shakhar (Shachar) which means:** <u>**Dawn or Morning**</u>. **Haylal (Lucifer) is the** <u>**son of the dawn**</u> **or the** <u>**son of the morning**</u> שַׁחַר **Shakhar (Shachar).** According the KJV bible Hebrew Strong's Concordance "**#<u>1966</u>, Lucifer means:** "**light-bearer", shining one, morning star"** or **the shining light.**"

89

CHILDREN OF THE MOST HIGH:
PRISTINE YOUTH AND FAMILY SOLUTIONS, LLC.
SONS AND DAUGHTERS OF THE MOST HIGH PUBLISHERS ®

OH, GRACIOUS MOST HIGH HEAVENLY FATHER, HOLY IS YOUR
NAME, YOUR WILL BE DONE NOW AND FOREVER!

According to the Online Gesenius' Hebrew-Chaldee Lexicon
(2020), **Lucifer (הֵילֵל Haylal, Hêylêl, Hay-lale'** is defined as:

הֵילֵל Isa. 14:12 according to LXX., Vulg., Targ.
Rabbin., Luth., *stella lucida, bright star*, i. e. *Lucifer*.
Nor is this a bad rendering, for there is added בֶּן־שָׁחַר
and in the Chaldee also Lucifer [the morning star],
is called כּוֹכַב נֹגְהָא, in Arab. زهر i. e. splendid star.
According to this opinion הֵילֵל would be derived from
the root הלל to shine; as a participial noun of the
conj. קִיטֵל, (comp. Arab. بيطر, Syr. صمحد and the
like), or else of a quadriliteral verb הילל, comp. הֵיכָל,
הֵידָד. However, הֵילֵל itself is not unfrequently Imper.
Hiph. of the verb יָלַל in the signification *wail, lament*
(Eze. 21:17; Zec. 11:2), and this does not appear
less suitable, and is adopted by Syr., Aqu. and
Jerome. ["This is less suitable." Ges. corr.]

90

THE DEVIL IS LUST, LIES, AND DELUSIONS; AND
THE MOST IS LOVE AND TRUTH WITHOUT CONFUSION!

CHILDREN OF THE MOST HIGH:
PRISTINE YOUTH AND FAMILY SOLUTIONS, LLC.
SONS AND DAUGHTERS OF THE MOST HIGH PUBLISHERS ®

OH, GRACIOUS MOST HIGH HEAVENLY FATHER, HOLY IS YOUR
NAME, YOUR WILL BE DONE NOW AND FOREVER!

According the KJV bible Hebrew Strong's Concordance
"**#<u>1966</u>, Satan שָׂטָן means: "adversary, one who withstands,
adversary (in general - personal or national), superhuman
adversary, an opponent; the arch-enemy of good.**"

CHILDREN OF THE MOST HIGH:
PRISTINE YOUTH AND FAMILY SOLUTIONS, LLC.
SONS AND DAUGHTERS OF THE MOST HIGH PUBLISHERS ®

OH, GRACIOUS MOST HIGH HEAVENLY FATHER, HOLY IS YOUR
NAME, YOUR WILL BE DONE NOW AND FOREVER!

According to the Online Gesenius' Hebrew-Chaldee Lexicon (2020), **satan** is defined as:

שָׂטָן — (1) *adversary* (Arabic شيطان), as in war, *an enemy*, 1 Ki. 5:18; 11:14, 23, 25; 1 Sam. 29:4; in a court of justice, Psa. 109:6 (compare Zec. 3:1, 2); and also whoever opposes himself to another, 2 Sam. 19:23; Nu. 22:22, "the angel of Jehovah stood in the way לְשָׂטָן לוֹ to resist him;" verse 32.

(2) With the art. הַשָּׂטָן (*adversary*, κατ' ἐξοχὴν) it assumes the nature of a pr. n. (see Hebr. Gramm., § 107, 2), and is *Satan, the devil*, the evil genius in the later theology of the Jews [rather, in the true revelation of God from the beginning], who seduces men (1 Chron. 21:1; in which place only it is without the article, compare 2 Samuel 24:1), and then accuses and calumniates them before God, Zech. 3:1, 2; Job 1:7; 2:2, seq.; compare Apoc. 12:10, ὁ κατήγωρ τῶν ἀδελφῶν ἡμῶν, ὁ κατηγορῶν αὐτῶν ἐνώπιον τοῦ θεοῦ ἡμῶν ἡμέρας καὶ νυκτός. But it is a groundless opinion of Alb. Schultens, Herder, and Eichhorn, that Satan, in the book of Job, is different from the Satan of the other books, and is a good angel employed to examine into the manners of men; and on this account, whenever in the early part of this book he is mentioned, they would read, הַשָּׂטָן i. e. περιοδευτής (from the root שׁוּט); this notion has now been rejected by all interpreters. And—

92

CHILDREN OF THE MOST HIGH:
PRISTINE YOUTH AND FAMILY SOLUTIONS, LLC.
SONS AND DAUGHTERS OF THE MOST HIGH PUBLISHERS ®

Also, be mindful that **Lucifer** existed before the language that we speak existed, **therefore; one of the evil one's greatest tools is modern day mistranslations and misinterpretations of the Most High Scriptures from their original languages and dialect in the pristine state they were originally revealed in**! For example: According the Online Merriam-Webster Dictionary (2020), **Hallel** is defined as: "a selection comprising Psalms 113–118 chanted during Jewish feasts (such as the Passover) **First Known use of Hallel 1702, in the meaning defined above History and Etymology for Hallel, Hebrew Hallēl meaning praise. Is Hallēl and Hêylêl the same word? Or are both words just similar in their appearance?**

In the KJV bible book of Isaiah chapter 14 verse 12. The same thing happens in the Quran. According to "(Blackler, Fischer, Lever, 2015), **Halal is denoting or relating to meat prepared as prescribed by Muslim law.**

93

CHILDREN OF THE MOST HIGH:
PRISTINE YOUTH AND FAMILY SOLUTIONS, LLC.
SONS AND DAUGHTERS OF THE MOST HIGH PUBLISHERS ®

In the Lane Arabic/English Lexicon (2003), the "**devil**" is referred to as **Haylal "The scape goat**," when he was in the Heavens. In the KJV bible book of Isaiah chapter 14 verse 12, is there a correlation between **Lucifer's** Aramic (Hebrew) names/titles of (הֵילֵל **Haylal, Hêylêl, Hay-lale'**) son of שַׁחַר **Shakhar (Shachar)** and the words: <u>Alleluia</u> and <u>Halleluiah</u> according to the bible? Unbeknown to many of us in the body of Christ, the word; "<u>**Halleluiah**</u>" **does not exist in the original Aramic (Hebrew) of the Old Testament of the bible or in the original Greek language of the New Testament bible.** The word <u>Halleluiah</u> exist in biblical commentaries and may exist in modern translations of the bible. However; the Greek word: "<u>Alleluia</u>" meaning "**praise ye JAH**" exists in the KJV bible book of Revelation chapter 19 verses 1, 3, 4, and 6 from the word <u>Halleluiah</u>.

CHILDREN OF THE MOST HIGH:
PRISTINE YOUTH AND FAMILY SOLUTIONS, LLC.
SONS AND DAUGHTERS OF THE MOST HIGH PUBLISHERS ®

Why does this matter? It matters because the root word of is "**Hallel**" and **Hêylêl** is **one of Lucifer's titles or names** as used in the aforementioned KJV bible book of Isaiah chapter 14 verse 12 in the original **Aramic (Hebrew)** language that this verse was originally revealed in. The being called **Lucifer, has many titles or names in Aramic (Hebrew), Syriac/Arabic, and in other languages** that describe the content of his character, his nature, and his actions!

For example: In the KJV bible book of **Revelation** chapter **12** verses **7-9**; it states: "And there was war in heaven: **Michael and his angels** fought against the **dragon**; and **the dragon fought and his angels** and prevailed not; neither was their place found any more in heaven. And the **great dragon** was cast out, that **old serpent, called the Devil, and Satan, which deceiveth the whole world**: he was cast out into the earth, and his **angels** were cast out with him."

95

THE DEVIL IS LUST, LIES, AND DELUSIONS; AND
THE MOST IS LOVE AND TRUTH WITHOUT CONFUSION!

CHILDREN OF THE MOST HIGH:
PRISTINE YOUTH AND FAMILY SOLUTIONS, LLC.
SONS AND DAUGHTERS OF THE MOST HIGH PUBLISHERS ®

OH, GRACIOUS MOST HIGH HEAVENLY FATHER, HOLY IS YOUR
NAME, YOUR WILL BE DONE NOW AND FOREVER!

So, in the aforementioned verses, one way that the devil
"**deceiveth the whole world**" was to make many people think
that **Satan, the dragon, the serpent,** and **Lucifer** (הֵילֵל **Haylal,
Hêylêl, Hay-lale'**) were different beings when the KJV bible
book of **Revelation** chapter **12** verses **7-9** makes it very clear
**that these names are titles that describes the same being, the
content of his character, his nature, and his actions!**

Therefore; unbeknown to many, the word: **Halleluiah** literally
means "**to praise Hallel (Lucifer)**" and "**Alleluia**" meaning
"**praise ye Jah (יָהּ Yahh)**". **When you put the letter "H" in
front of the word "Alleluia", it changes the meaning in the
Aramic (Hebrew) language**. This matters to the real followers
of Yashu'a Ha Mashiakh (Jesus the Messiah) because he said
in the KJV bible book of John chapter 8 verse 32: "And ye shall
know the truth, and the truth shall make you free." "Ye shall
know" (γινώσκω **ginōskō, is Strong's concordance #1097
and means to know, understand, perceive).**"

96

CHILDREN OF THE MOST HIGH:
PRISTINE YOUTH AND FAMILY SOLUTIONS, LLC.
SONS AND DAUGHTERS OF THE MOST HIGH PUBLISHERS ®

OH, GRACIOUS MOST HIGH HEAVENLY FATHER, HOLY IS YOUR
NAME, YOUR WILL BE DONE NOW AND FOREVER!

So, brothers and sisters, be not deceived by **the devil's delusion tool called "word games" of mistranslations of words in the bible** from their **original Aramic (Hebrew), Ashuric/Syriac (Arabic)** or **Greek** languages into other translated languages, such as words in **English** or other dialects or languages. **Outside of the word games of Scramble and the likes, words are not games and life and death are in the tongue!** In the KJV bible book of Psalms chapter 68 verse 4; it states **in the modern Hebrew script:**

שִׁירוּ לֵאלֹהִים זַמְּרוּ שְׁמוֹ סֹלּוּ לָרֹכֵב בָּעֲרָבוֹת בְּיָהּ שְׁמוֹ וְעִלְזוּ לְפָנָיו:

"Sing unto God, sing praises to his name: extol him that rideth upon the heavens by his name **JAH**, and rejoice before him."

According to the **Online Gesenius' Hebrew-Chaldee Lexicon** (2020), **JAH"** (יָהּ **Yahh**) is the KJV bible Hebrew Strong's Concordance "**#3050** and is defined as:

97

CHILDREN OF THE MOST HIGH:
PRISTINE YOUTH AND FAMILY SOLUTIONS, LLC.
SONS AND DAUGHTERS OF THE MOST HIGH PUBLISHERS ®

OH, GRACIOUS MOST HIGH HEAVENLY FATHER, HOLY IS YOUR
NAME, YOUR WILL BE DONE NOW AND FOREVER!

יָהּ *Jah* a word abbreviated from יְהֹוָה *Jehovah*,
or rather from the more ancient pronunciation יַהְוֹה
or יַהְוֶה [this rests on the *assumption* that one of
these contradictory pronunciations is the more an-
cient], whence by apocope יָהוּ (as יִשְׁתַּחוּ for יִשְׁתַּחֲוֶה)
then by the omission of the unaccented וּ, יָה, Lehrg.
157. Either of these forms is used promiscuously
at the end of many proper names, as אֵלִיָּהוּ, and אֵלִיָּה,
יִרְמְיָהוּ and יִרְמְיָה, יְשַׁעְיָהוּ and יְשַׁעְיָה, the final ה
in these compounds being always without Mappik.
יָהּ is principally used in certain customary phrases,
as הַלְלוּ־יָהּ "praise ye Jehovah!" Ps. 104:35; 105:
45; 106:1, 48; 111:1; 112:1; 113:1, etc. Besides
e. g. Ps. 89:9; 94:7, 12; Isa. 38:11; Ex. 15:2, עָזִּי
וְזִמְרָת יָהּ "my strength and my song is Jehovah."
Ps. 118:14; Isai. 12:2; Ps. 68:5, בְּיָהּ שְׁמוֹ "Jah is
his name" (comp. בְּ let. D). Isa. 26:4. (In a few
doxological forms this word is also retained in Syriac,
as ܬܶܫܒܽܘܚܬܳܐ ܠܡܳܪܝܳܐ glory to Jehovah, Assem. Bibl.
Orient. ii. 230; iii. 579.)

In the Lane Arabic/English Lexicon (2003), the "**devil**" is referred to as **Haylal** "**The scape goat**," when the he was in the Heavens. When the devil fell from grace, he was called: **Ibliys** "**Rebellious One**". When the devil was cast down to earth, he was called: **Azaazil** "**One Cast Down, Removed**", and also **Shaytaan**. The word **Shaytaan** stems from the verb **Shatana** which means "*a thing of clay*". "The word **Shaatan** from the same root, means "*the one who goes far from the truth; the wicked one*". When **Ibliys** took a body on Earth he became a **Shay** which means "*thing*", of **iyn** which means "**clay**" or "**a thing of clay**". The devil is also called: **Min Al Kaafireena** "**From those who conceal what they know to be true**". While on earth, the devil was called: **Jaan** "**Father of Jinn**", and **Jinn**. **Jinn** is a collective noun species of angels called **Cherubeems Jinniyyun** also, an **individual Jinn**). He was called: **Taaghuwt** "**to transgress, to stray**". Or **Taaghiya** derived from the verb: *Taghaa, Taaghuwt, is feminine and masculine, singular and plural, it does not change.*"

"Taaghiya "the one who transgressed", Noun: *Tughyaan means "transgression of limits."* Khannaas "To retreat to shrink; or to disappear, to get into hearts." *Derived from the verb Khanasa – to go back, disappear."* Satan and Lucifer are one and the same. They are both referred to as "the shining light" and "the son of dawn", which is the meaning of the word "Lucifer". On the Online Merriam-Webster Dictionary (2020), it defines the word: "dawn" as: "to begin to grow light as the sun rises." In the KJV bible book of Luke, chapter 18; it states: "I beheld Satan as lightning fall from heaven." In the KJV bible book of 2nd Corinthians chapter 11 verses 13-15; it states: "For such are false apostles, deceitful workers, transforming themselves into the apostles of Christ. And no marvel; for Satan himself is transformed into an angel of light. Therefore, it is no great thing if his ministers also be transformed as the ministers of righteousness; whose end shall be according to their works."

100

CHILDREN OF THE MOST HIGH:
PRISTINE YOUTH AND FAMILY SOLUTIONS, LLC.
SONS AND DAUGHTERS OF THE MOST HIGH PUBLISHERS ®

OH, GRACIOUS MOST HIGH HEAVENLY FATHER, HOLY IS YOUR
NAME, YOUR WILL BE DONE NOW AND FOREVER!

In the KJV bible book of Mathew chapter 7 verse 15; the Messiah Yashu'a (Jesus) said: "**Beware of false prophets, which come to you in sheep's clothing, but inwardly they are ravening wolves.**" So, it is imperative that the children of the Most High don't be deceived by the children of the devil and their <u>**wolves in sheep clothing**</u> or <u>**ministers of satan**</u> who preach and teach you about <u>**another Jesus**</u>, <u>**another spirit**</u>, and <u>**another gospel**</u> that sounds like the **doctrine of the Most High** that the Messiah Yashu'a (Jesus) and his beloved disciple **John son of Zebedee**, and is **brother James son of Zebedee (Sons of Thunder)** taught.

101

THE DEVIL IS LUST, LIES, AND DELUSIONS; AND
THE MOST IS LOVE AND TRUTH WITHOUT CONFUSION!

CHILDREN OF THE MOST HIGH:
PRISTINE YOUTH AND FAMILY SOLUTIONS, LLC.
SONS AND DAUGHTERS OF THE MOST HIGH PUBLISHERS ®

OH, GRACIOUS MOST HIGH HEAVENLY FATHER, HOLY IS YOUR
NAME, YOUR WILL BE DONE NOW AND FOREVER!

However, if a sincere-hearted person took the time to do a non-bias in-depth word by word study into the original languages of the literal words that the Messiah Yashu'a (Jesus) spoke; and compared it to what others say that he taught, unbeknown to many of us in the Body of Christ; **the Most High's Doctrine of Truth would easily differentiate itself from the many false doctrines that have <u>Lucifer and his angel messages as their root foundations</u>!** That's why in the KJV bible book of John chapter 8 verse 32; the Messiah Yashu'a (Jesus) said: "And <u>ye shall know</u> the truth, and the truth shall make you free." "<u>Ye shall know</u>" (γινώσκω **ginōskō,** is KJV bible Greek Strong's Concordance#1097 word: γινώσκω **ginōskō,** which means **to know, understand, perceive**)." In the KJV bible book of 2nd Corinthians chapter 11 verse 4; it states: "For if he that cometh **preacheth another Jesus**, whom we have not preached, or if ye **receive another spirit**, which ye have not received, **or another gospel**, which ye have not accepted, ye might well bear with him."

102

CHILDREN OF THE MOST HIGH:
PRISTINE YOUTH AND FAMILY SOLUTIONS, LLC.
SONS AND DAUGHTERS OF THE MOST HIGH PUBLISHERS ®

OH, GRACIOUS MOST HIGH HEAVENLY FATHER, HOLY IS YOUR
NAME, YOUR WILL BE DONE NOW AND FOREVER!

According to the Online American Heritage Dictionary (2020), the word "**Minister**" is from "Middle English **ministre**, from Old French, from Latin minister, meaning **servant**; to attend to the wants and needs of others: Volunteers ministered to the homeless after the flood." The first part of the word "**Minis**ter" is "**Minis**" which phonetically sounds exactly like the word "**Menace**", which are what the **Ministers of Satan** are; **trouble-makers**, not to be confused with the children of the Most High who Ad**minister** the Most High's doctrine to members of humanity. "According to the Online American Heritage Dictionary (2020), the word "**Menace**" from "Middle English manace, from Old French, from Late Latin minācia, sing. of Latin mināciae, threats, menaces, from mināx, mināc-, threatening, from minārī, to threaten, from minae, threats; a possible danger; a threat: a careless driver who was a menace to public safety. The quality of being threatening: a hint of menace in his voice."

103

CHILDREN OF THE MOST HIGH:
PRISTINE YOUTH AND FAMILY SOLUTIONS, LLC.
SONS AND DAUGHTERS OF THE MOST HIGH PUBLISHERS ®

"To constitute a threat to; endanger: A troublesome or annoying person: or considered her little brother to be a menace, tr.v. men·aced, men·ac·ing, men·ac·es." **Are angels being synonymous with good another delusion of the devil? Yes! Why**? Because you have **agreeable** and **disagreeable angelic-beings**. In the KJV bible book of **Revelation** chapter **12** verses **7-9**; it states: "And there was war in heaven: **Michael and his angels** (ἄγγελος **Angelos, meaning Messengers** according to the KJV bible Greek Strong's Concordance#32) fought against the **dragon**; and **the dragon fought and his angels** (ἄγγελος **Angelos, meaning Messengers**, according to the KJV bible Greek Strong's#32), and prevailed not; neither was their place found any more in heaven. And the **great dragon** was cast out, that **old serpent**, **called the Devil, and Satan**, which deceiveth the whole world: he was cast out into the earth, and his **angels** (ἄγγελος **Angelos, meaning Messengers**, according to the KJV bible Greek Strong's# 32) were cast out with him."

104

THE DEVIL IS LUST, LIES, AND DELUSIONS; AND
THE MOST IS LOVE AND TRUTH WITHOUT CONFUSION!

CHILDREN OF THE MOST HIGH:
PRISTINE YOUTH AND FAMILY SOLUTIONS, LLC.
SONS AND DAUGHTERS OF THE MOST HIGH PUBLISHERS ℗

OH, GRACIOUS MOST HIGH HEAVENLY FATHER, HOLY IS YOUR
NAME, YOUR WILL BE DONE NOW AND FOREVER!

In the aforementioned verses, the **great dragon** was cast out, that **old serpent**, **called the Devil, and Satan** are **titles of the same being**. So, in the Bible and in the Qur'aan/Qur'an or Koran; there are a diversity of titles for the being that is called: **"The Devil"** which **describes his actions, attributes, and true nature** which are also the same actions, attributes and true nature of the children of the devil. According to the KJV bible book of James chapter 2 verse 19 phrase **"the devils** (with a "**s**" on it)"**; does this mean that **"the devil** (without an "**s**" on it)" is **Leviathan** or one of a group or race of other beings who the bible refers to as "the devils"?**

The KJV bible book of James chapter 2 verse 19 states: "Thou (σὺ σύ sy) believest (πιστεύω pisteuō) that (ὅτι hoti) there is (ἐστί esti) one (εἷς heis) God (θεός theos) thou doest (ποιέω poieō) well (καλῶς kalōs) the devils (δαιμόνιον daimonion) also (καί kai) believe (πιστεύω pisteuō) and (καί kai) tremble (φρίσσω phrissō)."

105

CHILDREN OF THE MOST HIGH:
PRISTINE YOUTH AND FAMILY SOLUTIONS, LLC.
SONS AND DAUGHTERS OF THE MOST HIGH PUBLISHERS ®

OH, GRACIOUS MOST HIGH HEAVENLY FATHER, HOLY IS YOUR
NAME, YOUR WILL BE DONE NOW AND FOREVER!

"Thou believest that there is one God; thou doest well: the devils also believe, and tremble, (KJV bible book of James chapter 2 verse 19)." The KJV bible Greek Strong's Concordance#1140 phrase for **"the devils"** is "δαιμόνιον **daimonion.**" The phrase: "δαιμόνιον daimonion" is "<u>plural for evil spirits or the messengers and ministers of the devil.</u>" As it relates to the <u>**content of the character children of the devil**</u>, and the <u>**content of the character children of the Most High (God)**</u>; what are the **9 Deadly Venoms of the Desires of the great dragon, that old serpent called the devil and satan which deceiveth the whole world?**

106

CHILDREN OF THE MOST HIGH:
PRISTINE YOUTH AND FAMILY SOLUTIONS, LLC.
SONS AND DAUGHTERS OF THE MOST HIGH PUBLISHERS ®

In the KJV bible book of **Revelation** chapter **12** verses **7-9**; it states: "And there was war in heaven: **Michael and his angels** (ἄγγελος **Angelos, meaning Messengers** according to the KJV bible Greek Strong's Concordance#32) fought against the **dragon**; and **the dragon fought and his angels** (ἄγγελος **Angelos, meaning Messengers**, according to the KJV bible Greek Strong's#32), and prevailed not; neither was their place found any more in heaven. And the **great dragon** was cast out, that **old serpent**, **called the Devil, and Satan**, which deceiveth the whole world: he was cast out into the earth, and his **angels** (ἄγγελος **Angelos, meaning Messengers**, according to the KJV bible Greek Strong's# 32) were cast out with him.

Since angels are messengers, how does messages of the great dragon: that old serpent, called the Devil, and Satan, which deceiveth the whole world and his angels, and the **messages of Michael and his angels** relate to all members of humanity?

107

CHILDREN OF THE MOST HIGH:
PRISTINE YOUTH AND FAMILY SOLUTIONS, LLC.
SONS AND DAUGHTERS OF THE MOST HIGH PUBLISHERS ®

OH, GRACIOUS MOST HIGH HEAVENLY FATHER, HOLY IS YOUR
NAME, YOUR WILL BE DONE NOW AND FOREVER!

A person actions can sometime tell you more about them than their words. The great dragon: that old serpent, called the Devil, and Satan, which deceiveth the whole world and his angels (ἄγγελος **Angelos, meaning Messengers**), spread **messages** of **the 9 Deadly Venoms of the Desires of the great dragon: that old serpent, called the Devil, and Satan**, which are: **Slothful, Wrath, Pride, Greed, Lust, Hopeless Fear Disobedience, Lying, Heinous Murder**, and **Wickedness**.

108

CHILDREN OF THE MOST HIGH:
PRISTINE YOUTH AND FAMILY SOLUTIONS, LLC.
SONS AND DAUGHTERS OF THE MOST HIGH PUBLISHERS ®

OH, GRACIOUS MOST HIGH HEAVENLY FATHER, HOLY IS YOUR
NAME, YOUR WILL BE DONE NOW AND FOREVER!

The **9 Deadly Venoms of the Desires of the great dragon: that old serpent, called the Devil, and Satan** are also the **Devil's Poison Fruits of the Spirit of Negative Character-Building Essentials for the children of the devil**. The messages of the **Arch Angelic-Being Miykaa'iyl (Michael) and his angels** (ἄγγελος Angelos) are advocates of the **9X9 True Vine** (Yashu'a, Jesus) **Fruits of the Spirit of Positive Character-Building Essentials for the children of the Most High** which are the characteristics of: **love**, **joy**, **peace**, **longsuffering** (μακροθυμία makrothymía, patience, endurance, constancy, steadfastness, perseverance), **gentleness**, **goodness**, **faith**, **meekness** (πραότης praotēs, humility), and **temperance** (ἐγκράτεια enkráteia, self-control). In the KJV bible book of John chapter 14 verse 6; Yashu'a (Jesus) saith unto him, **"I am the way, the truth, and the life: no man cometh unto the Father, but by me."**

109

THE DEVIL IS LUST, LIES, AND DELUSIONS; AND
THE MOST IS LOVE AND TRUTH WITHOUT CONFUSION!

CHILDREN OF THE MOST HIGH:
PRISTINE YOUTH AND FAMILY SOLUTIONS, LLC.
SONS AND DAUGHTERS OF THE MOST HIGH PUBLISHERS ®

OH, GRACIOUS MOST HIGH HEAVENLY FATHER, HOLY IS YOUR
NAME, YOUR WILL BE DONE NOW AND FOREVER!

The messages of the **Arch Angelic-Being Miykaa'iyl
(Michael) and his angels** (ἄγγελος Angelos) are to obey **the
Most High (ELYOWN עֶלְיוֹן EL אֵל) ONLY!!!** In the KJV
bible book of Matthew chapter 22 verses 37-38; Yashu'a
(Jesus) said unto him: **"Thou shalt love the Lord thy God with
all thy heart, and with all thy soul, and with all thy mind.
This is the first and great commandment."**

Therefore, each person on the planet earth is either a knowing
or unknowing advocate of the **messages of the great dragon,
that old serpent called the devil and satan** which deceiveth
the whole world **or an advocate of the messages of the Arch
Angelic-Being Miykaa'iyl (Micha-El-means who dares to be
like the Most High (ELYOWN עֶלְיוֹן EL אֵל)** by the purpose of
why and how they live their lives, the way they think, the way
they speak, their actions and deeds.

110

CHILDREN OF THE MOST HIGH:
PRISTINE YOUTH AND FAMILY SOLUTIONS, LLC.
SONS AND DAUGHTERS OF THE MOST HIGH PUBLISHERS ℠

OH, GRACIOUS MOST HIGH HEAVENLY FATHER, HOLY IS YOUR
NAME, YOUR WILL BE DONE NOW AND FOREVER!

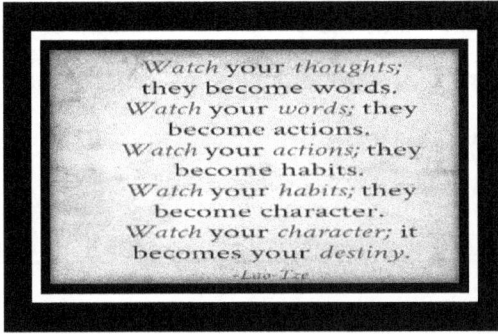

Watch your *thoughts;*
they become words.
Watch your *words;* they
become actions.
Watch your *actions;* they
become habits.
Watch your *habits;* they
become character.
Watch your *character;* it
becomes your *destiny.*
-Lao-Tze

The aforementioned is for the children of the Most High to
beware of and to put into moment to moment action to best be
able to prevent being deceived by the devil's lust, lies and
delusions while simultaneously being empowered, inspired,
and guided from moment to moment by the Most High's love
and truth without confusion!

111

THE DEVIL IS LUST, LIES, AND DELUSIONS; AND THE MOST IS LOVE AND TRUTH WITHOUT CONFUSION!

CHILDREN OF THE MOST HIGH:
PRISTINE YOUTH AND FAMILY SOLUTIONS, LLC.
SONS AND DAUGHTERS OF THE MOST HIGH PUBLISHERS ®

OH, GRACIOUS MOST HIGH HEAVENLY FATHER, HOLY IS YOUR NAME, YOUR WILL BE DONE NOW AND FOREVER!

More information about the **9 Deadly Venoms of the Desires of the great dragon, that old serpent called the devil and satan which deceiveth the whole world, and the 9X9 True Vine** (Yashu'a, Jesus) <u>**Fruits of the Spirit of Positive Character-Building Essentials for the children of the Most High**</u> can be acquired in the book entitled: **"Spiritual Trillionaire! Cherishing the Breath of Life while Simultaneously Preparing for the Blow of Death!"** on Amazon or on <u>**childrenofthemosthigh.com**</u>.

112

CHILDREN OF THE MOST HIGH:
PRISTINE YOUTH AND FAMILY SOLUTIONS, LLC.
SONS AND DAUGHTERS OF THE MOST HIGH PUBLISHERS ®

OH, GRACIOUS MOST HIGH HEAVENLY FATHER, HOLY IS YOUR
NAME, YOUR WILL BE DONE NOW AND FOREVER!

Chapter 4: Expound on the 9X9 True Vine (Yashu'a, Jesus) B.A.-K.A.-R.E.(RAY)?

*In the KJV bible book of Mark chapter 7 verses 7; 21-23; Yashu'a (Jesus) said: "Howbeit in vain do they worship me, teaching for doctrines the commandments of men (ἄνθρωπος anthrōpos (**male or female human being**) – KJV Greek Strong's Concordance #444). For from within, out of the* heart *of men [**human beings, ἄνθρωπος anthrōpos**], proceed evil thoughts, adulteries, fornications, murders, Thefts, covetousness, wickedness, deceit, lasciviousness, an evil eye, blasphemy, pride, foolishness. All these evil things come from within, and defile the man (ἄνθρωπος anthrōpos (**male or female human being**) – KJV Greek Strong's Concordance #444)."*

113

CHILDREN OF THE MOST HIGH:
PRISTINE YOUTH AND FAMILY SOLUTIONS, LLC.
SONS AND DAUGHTERS OF THE MOST HIGH PUBLISHERS ®

OH, GRACIOUS MOST HIGH HEAVENLY FATHER, HOLY IS YOUR NAME, YOUR WILL BE DONE NOW AND FOREVER!

> Oh, Children of the Most High,
> Repent to the Most and
> turn away from
> **DISOBEDIENCE FOREVER!**

In order for the Children of the Most High; Pristine Youth and Family Solutions LLC. to be obedient to the Most High Heavenly Father, we seek to be positive difference makers who helps and teach youth and adults: how to apply the doctrine of the Most High through the **True Vine "Yashu'a" (Jesus) B.A.-K.A.-R.E. Sequential Order of Learning** in all that they aspire to do. We also seek to teach them how to create positive predetermined goals, how to achieve positive success according to what positive success means to them, how to achieve positive happiness according to what positive happiness means to them, and how to learn to work together with members of humanity to create a world where all youth and all adults who are children of the Most High are happy, healthy, and balanced mentally, spiritually, physically, emotionally, financially, personally, professionally, and socially.

114

CHILDREN OF THE MOST HIGH:
PRISTINE YOUTH AND FAMILY SOLUTIONS, LLC.
SONS AND DAUGHTERS OF THE MOST HIGH PUBLISHERS ®

OH, GRACIOUS MOST HIGH HEAVENLY FATHER, HOLY IS YOUR
NAME, YOUR WILL BE DONE NOW AND FOREVER!

What are the 9 Children of the Most High: Pristine Youth
and Family Solutions, LLC. 9X9 True Vine (Yashu'a,
Jesus) "B.A.-K.A.-R.E. Sequential Order of Learning
Habits of Success?

1). The 9 True Vine (Yashu'a, Jesus) Mind Gardening
   Memorization Keys to Success.
2). The 9 True Vine (Yashu'a, Jesus) Elements of
   Healthy Living.
3). The 9 True Vine (Yashu'a, Jesus) Attributes as
   Habits of Success.
4). The 9 True Vine (Yashu'a, Jesus) Mental
   Transformation Principles.
5). The 9 True Vine (Yashu'a, Jesus) Spiritual Gifts.
6). The 9 True Vine (Yashu'a, Jesus) Titles of Divinity.
7). The 9 True Vine (Yashu'a, Jesus) Fruits of the Spirit
   of Positive Character-Building Essentials.
8). The 9 True Vine (Yashu'a, Jesus) Work Ethics.
9). The 9 True Vine (Yashu'a, Jesus) Values.

115

CHILDREN OF THE MOST HIGH:
PRISTINE YOUTH AND FAMILY SOLUTIONS, LLC.
SONS AND DAUGHTERS OF THE MOST HIGH PUBLISHERS ✲

OH, GRACIOUS MOST HIGH HEAVENLY FATHER, HOLY IS YOUR
NAME, YOUR WILL BE DONE NOW AND FOREVER!

What is **the Children of the Most High: Pristine Youth and Family Solutions, LLC. 9X9 True Vine (Yashu'a, Jesus) B.A.-K.A.-R.E. Sequential Order of Learning?**

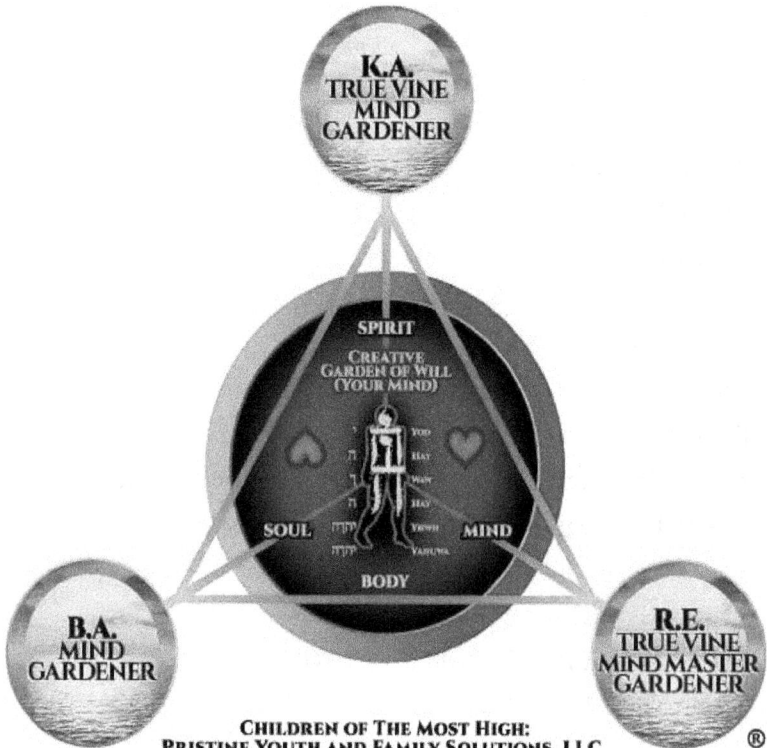

CHILDREN OF THE MOST HIGH:
PRISTINE YOUTH AND FAMILY SOLUTIONS, LLC.
9X9 TRUE VINE "YASHU'A" (JESUS) B.A.-K.A.-R.E.
SEQUENTIAL ORDER OF LEARNING®

116

THE DEVIL IS LUST, LIES, AND DELUSIONS; AND
THE MOST IS LOVE AND TRUTH WITHOUT CONFUSION!

CHILDREN OF THE MOST HIGH:
PRISTINE YOUTH AND FAMILY SOLUTIONS, LLC.
SONS AND DAUGHTERS OF THE MOST HIGH PUBLISHERS ®

OH, GRACIOUS MOST HIGH HEAVENLY FATHER, HOLY IS YOUR
NAME, YOUR WILL BE DONE NOW AND FOREVER!

The KJV bible book of **Psalms chapter 84 verse 11**; with **Hebrew (Aramic)** inserts states:

Psalms (KJV) 84:11 with **Hebrew inserts**:

כִּי שֶׁמֶשׁ וּמָגֵן יְהוָה אֱלֹהִים חֵן וְכָבוֹד יִתֵּן יְהוָה לֹא
יִמְנַע־טוֹב לַהֹלְכִים בְּתָמִים:

In the KJV bible book of **Psalms chapter 84 verse 11**; it states: "For the LORD (**Yĕhovah, יְהוָה, Yahuwa**) **God** (**Elohiym אֱלֹהִים**) is a "**Sun**" **Shemesh שֶׁמֶשׁ** and "**Shield**" **Magen מָגֵן**: the **LORD** (**Yĕhovah, Yahuwa**) will give grace and glory: no good thing will he withhold from them that walk uprightly **Tamiym תָּמִים**." The "**Sun**" (**RE**) is the light as a star that sustains all life on the planet earth.

117

CHILDREN OF THE MOST HIGH:
PRISTINE YOUTH AND FAMILY SOLUTIONS, LLC.
SONS AND DAUGHTERS OF THE MOST HIGH PUBLISHERS ®

OH, GRACIOUS MOST HIGH HEAVENLY FATHER, HOLY IS YOUR
NAME, YOUR WILL BE DONE NOW AND FOREVER!

In the **True Vine (Yashu'a, Jesus) B.A.-K.A.-R.E.** Sequential
Order of Learning, the **RE (Sun)** connects to the body as the light
(**RE**) that shines in the **darkness (Body)** that the **darkness (Body)**
does not comprehend in the KJV bible book of John chapter 1
verse 5; as **Yashu'a (Jesus)** said in the KJV bible book of
Matthew chapter 6 verse 22 "the light (**RE**) of the body is the
eye: if therefore thine eye be single, thy whole body shall be
full of light." **B.A.** is **Ancient African** for "**Soul**", and **K.A.** is
Ancient African for "**Spirit**". So, "**B.A.-K.A.-R.E.**" translates in
English as: **The Soul and Spirit, Sun-Light of Life of Yĕhovah,
Yahuwa, Yahweh, Yahovah, Jehovah (Lord God),** and
Yahayyu in Modern Hebrew translates as **Existing One** or **Living
One** that sustains all life on the planet earth, and it also translates
as: "**Glorious is the Spirit of the Lord God (RE).**" The acronyms
of "**B.A.-K.A.-R.E.**" in **English** stands for: Become, Aware,
Knowledge, Apply, Reflect, Experience. **Yashu'a (Jesus)** is the
Rabboni (Master ραββονί Rhabbouni – KJV Strong's Greek
Lexicon#4462) of the **B.A.-K.A.-R.E. Sequential Order of
Learning!**

CHILDREN OF THE MOST HIGH:
PRISTINE YOUTH AND FAMILY SOLUTIONS, LLC.
SONS AND DAUGHTERS OF THE MOST HIGH PUBLISHERS ®

OH, GRACIOUS MOST HIGH HEAVENLY FATHER, HOLY IS YOUR
NAME, YOUR WILL BE DONE NOW AND FOREVER!

Therefore, the **True Vine (Yashu'a, Jesus) B.A.-K.A.-R.E.**
Sequential Order of Learning youth and adult learners
Become **A**ware of the meaning of the KJV bible book of Hosea
chapter 4 verse 6: "My people (children of the Most High) are
being destroyed for lack of not knowing **God's (אלהים**
Elôhîym) A.W.A.R.E. knowledge." As the **Children of the**
Most High Pristine Youth and Family Solutions, LLC. 9X9
True Vine (Yashu'a, Jesus) B.A.-K.A.-R.E. Sequential
Order of **Learning** continues to be applied and practiced over
time by youth and adult learners, opportunities will occur for
them to **R**eflect on their **E**xperiences as they share and process
what they learned with others; in an ongoing process that may
help youth and adults who are children of the Most High to
develop new skills that enables them to best respond to daily
life situations that will lead to successful outcomes.

119

CHILDREN OF THE MOST HIGH:
PRISTINE YOUTH AND FAMILY SOLUTIONS, LLC.
SONS AND DAUGHTERS OF THE MOST HIGH PUBLISHERS ®

OH, GRACIOUS MOST HIGH HEAVENLY FATHER, HOLY IS YOUR
NAME, YOUR WILL BE DONE NOW AND FOREVER!

This also affords youth and adults who are children of the Most
High, opportunities to create new ways of how to utilize their
newly acquired knowledge to successfully achieve all of their
positive life aspirations and predetermined positive goals.

CHILDREN OF THE MOST HIGH:
PRISTINE YOUTH AND FAMILY SOLUTIONS, LLC.
SONS AND DAUGHTERS OF THE MOST HIGH PUBLISHERS ®

OH, GRACIOUS MOST HIGH HEAVENLY FATHER, HOLY IS YOUR
NAME, YOUR WILL BE DONE NOW AND FOREVER!

By learning **God's (אלהים Elôhîym) All Wise Abundant Right**
Exact (A.W.A.R.E) Knowledge with a sincere-heart and
focused mind, they acquire the **God's (אלהים Elôhîym) All**
Wise Abundant Right Exact (A.W.A.R.E) Knowledge which
affords youth and adult learners who are children of the Most
High the opportunity to **A**pply **God's (אלהים Elôhîym)**
A.W.A.R.E. knowledge in order to receive the mental, spiritual
and physical (mind, body, spirit, and soul), benefits in the
process of experiencing God's love and truth without
confusion.

Therefore; the aforementioned is for the children of the Most
High to beware of and to put into moment to moment action to
best be able to prevent being deceived by the devil's lust, lies
and delusions while simultaneously being empowered,
inspired, and guided from moment to moment by the Most
High's love and truth without confusion!

121

CHILDREN OF THE MOST HIGH:
PRISTINE YOUTH AND FAMILY SOLUTIONS, LLC.
SONS AND DAUGHTERS OF THE MOST HIGH PUBLISHERS *

OH, GRACIOUS MOST HIGH HEAVENLY FATHER, HOLY IS YOUR
NAME, YOUR WILL BE DONE NOW AND FOREVER!

Chapter 5: Frenemy, Munaafiqiyn be on your Guard, so that the Judas Effect won't leave you Prematurely dead in the Grave Yard!

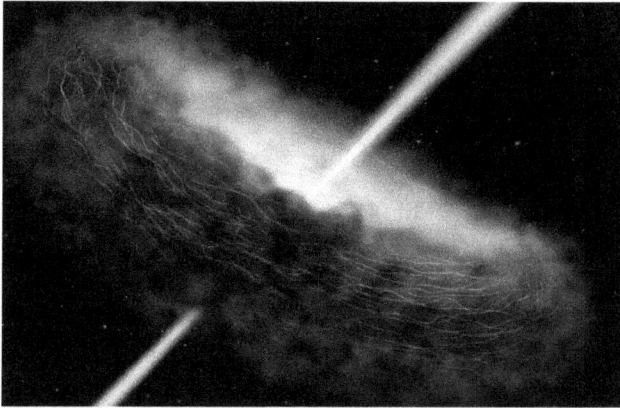

In the KJV bible book of Psalms chapter 109 verses 2-5; it states: "For the mouth of the wicked and the mouth of the deceitful are opened against me: they have spoken against me with a lying tongue. They compassed me about also with words of hatred; and fought against me without a cause. For my love they are my adversaries: but I [give myself unto] prayer. And they have rewarded me evil for good, and hatred for my love."

122

CHILDREN OF THE MOST HIGH:
PRISTINE YOUTH AND FAMILY SOLUTIONS, LLC.
SONS AND DAUGHTERS OF THE MOST HIGH PUBLISHERS ®

OH, GRACIOUS MOST HIGH HEAVENLY FATHER, HOLY IS YOUR
NAME, YOUR WILL BE DONE NOW AND FOREVER!

The devil is sin, and sin is unjust; the Most High is "The
Loving" and "The Just"! Define Frenemy, Munaafiqiyn, and
the Judas Effect? Munaafiqiyn is an Ashuric/Syriac
(Arabic) word that means: hypocrites. The word: "Arabic"
derived from the root word: "Araba (عَرَبَ) " which means:
"vehicle or mobile". Munaafiqiyn are children of the devil.
Munaafiqiyn are people who become aware of the Most High's
truth, and are the ones who cover the facts; it is the same for
them, whether you warn them, or do not warn them; they are
not going to be faithful to the Most High Heavenly Father.
When they meet those, who have faith in the Most High, they
say: "we have faith also"; and when they get back with their
children of the devil friends, they say: "surely we are with you,
we were only ridiculing them."

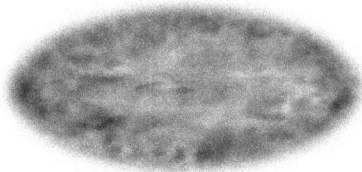

123

CHILDREN OF THE MOST HIGH:
PRISTINE YOUTH AND FAMILY SOLUTIONS, LLC.
SONS AND DAUGHTERS OF THE MOST HIGH PUBLISHERS ®

Yashu'a (Jesus) spoke about them in the KJV bible book of John chapter 12 verses 48-50, where he said: "He that rejected me, and receiveth not my words, hath one that judgeth him: the word that I have spoken, the same shall judge him in the last day. For I have not spoken of myself; but the Father which sent me, he gave me a commandment, what I should say, and what I should speak." And I know that his commandment is life everlasting: whatsoever I speak therefore, even as the Father said unto me, so I speak."

"According to the Online Merriam-Webster Dictionary (2020), **"hypocrites (Munaafiqiyn)** means: people who acts in contradiction to his or her stated opinions. **Frenemy** means: one who pretends to be a friend but is actually an enemy. **Judas** is defined as: the disciple who in the Gospel accounts, who betrayed Jesus. "**Effect** means: a condition or occurrence traceable to a cause."

CHILDREN OF THE MOST HIGH:
PRISTINE YOUTH AND FAMILY SOLUTIONS, LLC.
SONS AND DAUGHTERS OF THE MOST HIGH PUBLISHERS ®

OH, GRACIOUS MOST HIGH HEAVENLY FATHER, HOLY IS YOUR
NAME, YOUR WILL BE DONE NOW AND FOREVER!

So, the "**Judas Effect**" _is a condition or occurrence traceable to a cause of being betrayed by a person or people who pretends to be a friend but is actually an enemy._ Since we are influenced by the people, we surround ourselves with the most; do you surround yourself the most with people that do what is right according to the Most High? Or do you predominately surround yourself with people that do not do what is right in according to the Most High? What are the natures and content of character of the people that you surround yourself with the most?

125

THE DEVIL IS LUST, LIES, AND DELUSIONS; AND
THE MOST IS LOVE AND TRUTH WITHOUT CONFUSION!

CHILDREN OF THE MOST HIGH:
PRISTINE YOUTH AND FAMILY SOLUTIONS, LLC.
SONS AND DAUGHTERS OF THE MOST HIGH PUBLISHERS ®

OH, GRACIOUS MOST HIGH HEAVENLY FATHER, HOLY IS YOUR
NAME, YOUR WILL BE DONE NOW AND FOREVER!

Would you or the people you surround yourself with the most, be afraid if all of you looked in the mirror, and was only able to see the reflection of your true nature and the true contents of your character instead of your face?

John 15

12 "This is my commandment, that you love one another as I have loved you.

13 Greater love has no one than this, that someone lay down his life for his friends.

126

THE DEVIL IS LUST, LIES, AND DELUSIONS; AND
THE MOST IS LOVE AND TRUTH WITHOUT CONFUSION!

CHILDREN OF THE MOST HIGH:
PRISTINE YOUTH AND FAMILY SOLUTIONS, LLC.
SONS AND DAUGHTERS OF THE MOST HIGH PUBLISHERS ®

OH, GRACIOUS MOST HIGH HEAVENLY FATHER, HOLY IS YOUR
NAME, YOUR WILL BE DONE NOW AND FOREVER!

Always know, and always remember that true friends come free and true! The aforementioned is for the children of the Most High to beware of and to put into moment-to-moment action to best be able to prevent being deceived by the devil's lust, lies, and delusions; while simultaneously being empowered, inspired, and guided from moment to moment by the Most High's love and truth without confusion!

CHILDREN OF THE MOST HIGH:
PRISTINE YOUTH AND FAMILY SOLUTIONS, LLC.
SONS AND DAUGHTERS OF THE MOST HIGH PUBLISHERS ®

OH, GRACIOUS MOST HIGH HEAVENLY FATHER, HOLY IS YOUR
NAME, YOUR WILL BE DONE NOW AND FOREVER!

Have you ever wondered why spiders don't get stuck in their own webs?

THE DEVIL'S WEB

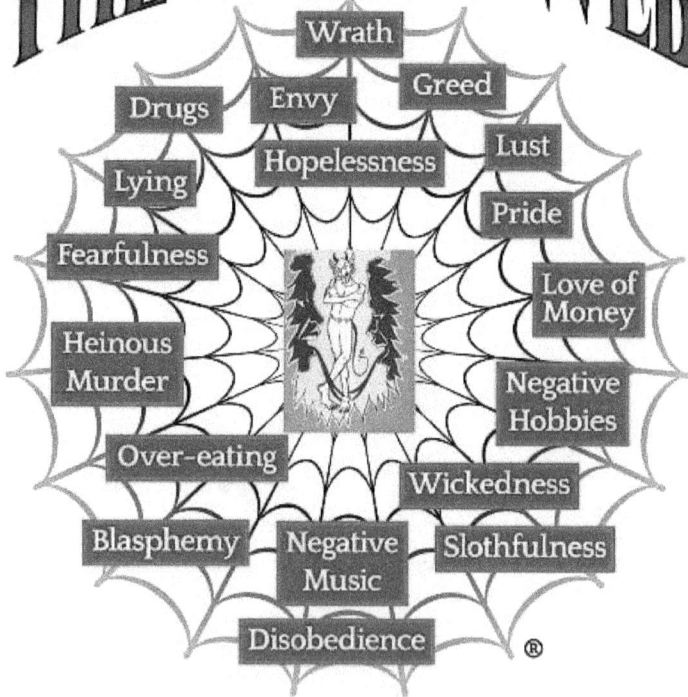

Wrath

Envy

Greed

Drugs

Hopelessness

Lust

Lying

Fearfulness

Pride

Love of Money

Heinous Murder

Negative Hobbies

Over-eating

Wickedness

Blasphemy

Negative Music

Slothfulness

Disobedience ®

CHILDREN OF THE MOST HIGH:
PRISTINE YOUTH AND FAMILY SOLUTIONS, LLC.
SONS AND DAUGHTERS OF THE MOST HIGH PUBLISHERS ®

OH, GRACIOUS MOST HIGH HEAVENLY FATHER, HOLY IS YOUR
NAME, YOUR WILL BE DONE NOW AND FOREVER!

**According to the bible, who are the children of the Most
High** (God)? **And who are the children of the devil?** In the
KJV bible book of Genesis chapter 3 verse 15; it states: "And I
will put **enmity (hatred)** between thee and the woman, and
between thy **seed (Zera`, זֶרַע)** and her **seed (Zera`, זֶרַע)**; it shall
bruise thy head, and thou shalt bruise his heel." It is important
to know that according to the bible, <u>there are two separate</u>
<u>children on the planet earth</u>; <u>the children of the Most High</u>
who are referred to as **Eve's seed (physical children)** and <u>the</u>
<u>children of the devil</u> **(physical children)** referred to as the
serpent's seed (Zera`, זֶרַע). The **KJV bible Hebrew Strong's
Concordance#2233 word for "seed" is "Zera" זֶרַע,** which
means: **seed, semen virile, child, carnally, fruitful, physical
offspring, descendants, posterity, children, sowing, or
physical children)."**

129

CHILDREN OF THE MOST HIGH:
PRISTINE YOUTH AND FAMILY SOLUTIONS, LLC.
SONS AND DAUGHTERS OF THE MOST HIGH PUBLISHERS ®

In the KJV bible book of Isaiah chapter 14 verse 16; it refers to **Lucifer** as **a man**: "How art thou fallen from heaven, O **Lucifer**; is this **the man** that made the earth to tremble, that did shake kingdoms." In the KJV bible book of Revelation chapter 13 verse 18; it states: "Here is wisdom. Let him that hath understanding count the **number of the beast**: **for it is the number of a man**; and his number is Six hundred threescore and six [**666**]." In the KJV bible book of 1st John chapter 3 verses 9-10; it states: "Whosoever is born of God doeth not commit sin; for his **seed** remained in him: and he cannot sin, because he is born of God. In this **the children of God** are manifest, and **the children of the devil:** whosoever doeth not righteousness is not of God, neither he that loveth not his brother."

130

CHILDREN OF THE MOST HIGH:
PRISTINE YOUTH AND FAMILY SOLUTIONS, LLC.
SONS AND DAUGHTERS OF THE MOST HIGH PUBLISHERS ®

According to the bible, are people born wicked?

Yes! In the KJV bible book of Psalms chapter 58 verses 3-5; it states: "<u>**The wicked are estranged from the womb. The KJV bible Hebrew Strong's Concordance #7358 for the word "estranged" is:** רֶחֶם **rechem meaning from the womb of a woman**</u>), <u>**they go astray as soon as they be born, speaking lies.**</u> Their <u>**poison is like the poison of a serpent:**</u> **they are like the deaf adder that stoppeth her ear; which will not hearken to the voice of charmers, charming never so wisely.**" In the KJV bible book of 1st John chapter 3 verses 9-10; it states: **"Whosoever is born of God doth not commit sin; for his seed remained in him: and he cannot sin, because he is born of God. <u>In this the children of God are manifest,</u> <u>and the children of the devil</u>: whosoever doeth not righteousness is not of God, neither he that loveth not his brother."**

CHILDREN OF THE MOST HIGH;
PRISTINE YOUTH AND FAMILY SOLUTIONS, LLC.
SONS AND DAUGHTERS OF THE MOST HIGH PUBLISHERS ®

OH, GRACIOUS MOST HIGH HEAVENLY FATHER, HOLY IS YOUR
NAME, YOUR WILL BE DONE NOW AND FOREVER!

So, **the content of the character of the children of the devil** are the **9 Deadly Venoms of the Desires of the great dragon, that old serpent called the devil and satan which deceiveth the whole world** which **can lead to a person getting deceived by the devil's lust, lies, and delusions that causes the mind and heart much confusion**! What are **9 Deadly Venoms of Desires of the great dragon, that old serpent called the devil and satan which deceiveth the whole world?** The **9 Deadly Venoms of Desires are: Slothful, Wrath, Pride, Greed, Lust, Hopeless Fear Disobedience, Lying, Heinous Murder, and Wickedness.** In the KJV bible book of **Revelation** chapter **12** verses **7-9**; it states: "And there was war in heaven: **Michael and his angels** (ἄγγελος **Angelos, meaning Messengers** according to the KJV bible Greek Strong's Concordance#32) fought against the **dragon**; and **the dragon fought and his angels** (ἄγγελος **Angelos, meaning Messengers**, according to the KJV bible Greek Strong's#32), And prevailed not; neither was their place found any more in heaven."

132

CHILDREN OF THE MOST HIGH:
PRISTINE YOUTH AND FAMILY SOLUTIONS, LLC.
SONS AND DAUGHTERS OF THE MOST HIGH PUBLISHERS ®

OH, GRACIOUS MOST HIGH HEAVENLY FATHER, HOLY IS YOUR
NAME, YOUR WILL BE DONE NOW AND FOREVER!

"And the **great dragon** was cast out, that **old serpent, called the Devil, and Satan,** which deceiveth the whole world: he was cast out into the earth, and his **angels** (ἄγγελος Angelos, **meaning Messengers,** according to the KJV bible Greek Strong's# 32) were cast out with him." **Since angels are messengers, how does messages of the great dragon: that old serpent, called the Devil, and Satan, which deceiveth the whole world and his angels** and the **messages of Michael and his angels** relate to all members of humanity? The great dragon: that old serpent, called the Devil, and Satan, which deceiveth the whole world and his angels (ἄγγελος **Angelos, meaning Messengers**), spread **messages** of the 9 Deadly Venoms of the Desires of the great dragon: that old serpent, called the Devil, and Satan, which are: **Slothful, Wrath, Pride, Greed, Lust, Hopeless Fear Disobedience, Lying, Heinous Murder,** and **Wickedness.**

133

CHILDREN OF THE MOST HIGH:
PRISTINE YOUTH AND FAMILY SOLUTIONS, LLC.
SONS AND DAUGHTERS OF THE MOST HIGH PUBLISHERS ®

The messages of **Michael and his angels** (ἄγγελος Angelos) are in the KJV bible book of Hebrews chapter 8 verses 10-14; states: **"For this is the covenant that I will make with the house of Israel after those days, saith the Lord; I will put my laws into their mind, and write them in their hearts: and I will be to them a God, and they shall be to me a people. And they shall not teach every man his neighbour, and every man his brother, saying, Know the Lord: for all shall know me, from the least to the greatest. For I will be merciful to their unrighteousness, and their sins and their iniquities will I remember no more. In that he saith, a new covenant, he hath made the first old. Now that which decayeth and waxeth old is ready to vanish away."** In the KJV bible book of Revelation chapter 22 verses 14-16; Yashu'a (Jesus) saith "Blessed are they that do his commandments, that they may have right to the tree of life, and may enter in through the gates into the city."

134

CHILDREN OF THE MOST HIGH:
PRISTINE YOUTH AND FAMILY SOLUTIONS, LLC.
SONS AND DAUGHTERS OF THE MOST HIGH PUBLISHERS ®

OH, GRACIOUS MOST HIGH HEAVENLY FATHER, HOLY IS YOUR
NAME, YOUR WILL BE DONE NOW AND FOREVER!

In the KJV bible book of John chapter 14 verse 6; Yashu'a (Jesus) saith unto him, "I am the way, the truth, and the life: no man cometh unto the Father, but by me." In the KJV bible book of Matthew chapter 22 verses 37-38; Yashu'a (Jesus) said unto him: "Thou shalt love the Lord thy God with all thy heart, and with all thy soul, and with all thy mind. This is the first and great commandment." Sometimes, a person actions, speaks louder than their words.

Therefore; **REMEMBER**: each person on the planet earth is either a knowing or an unknowing advocate of the **messages of the great dragon, that old serpent called the devil and satan** which deceiveth the whole world **or an advocate of the messages of the Arch Angelic-Being Miykaa'iyl (Micha-El-means who dares to be like the Most High (ELYOWN עֶלְיוֹן EL אֵל**) by the purpose of why and how they live their lives, the way they think, the way they speak, their actions and deeds.

135

THE DEVIL IS LUST, LIES, AND DELUSIONS; AND THE MOST IS LOVE AND TRUTH WITHOUT CONFUSION!

CHILDREN OF THE MOST HIGH:
PRISTINE YOUTH AND FAMILY SOLUTIONS, LLC.
SONS AND DAUGHTERS OF THE MOST HIGH PUBLISHERS ®

OH, GRACIOUS MOST HIGH HEAVENLY FATHER, HOLY IS YOUR NAME, YOUR WILL BE DONE NOW AND FOREVER!

So, the **content of the character of the children of the Most High** are the 9 Children of the Most High: Pristine Youth and Family Solutions, LLC. 9X9 True Vine (Yashu'a, Jesus) B.A.-K.A.-R.E. Sequential Order of Learning Habits of Success!

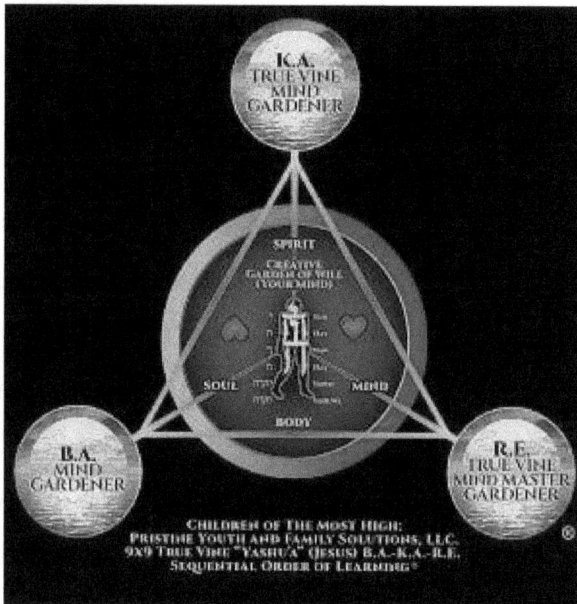

136

CHILDREN OF THE MOST HIGH:
PRISTINE YOUTH AND FAMILY SOLUTIONS, LLC.
SONS AND DAUGHTERS OF THE MOST HIGH PUBLISHERS ®

OH, GRACIOUS MOST HIGH HEAVENLY FATHER, HOLY IS YOUR
NAME, YOUR WILL BE DONE NOW AND FOREVER!

Chapter 6: Lust, Pornography, Sorcery, and Witchcraft are some of the Devil and the Children of Devil Master Tools of Deception!

In the KJV bible book of John chapter 8 verse 44; the Messiah Yashu'a (Jesus) said: "*Ye are of your father the devil, and the lusts of your father ye will do. He was a murderer from the beginning, and abode not in the truth, because there is no truth in him. When he speaketh a lie, he speaketh of his own: for he is a liar, and the father of it.*"

137

CHILDREN OF THE MOST HIGH:
PRISTINE YOUTH AND FAMILY SOLUTIONS, LLC.
SONS AND DAUGHTERS OF THE MOST HIGH PUBLISHERS ®

In the KJV bible book of Revelation chapter 17 verse 5; it states: "And upon her forehead was a name written, **MYSTERY, BABYLON THE GREAT, THE MOTHER OF HARLOTS AND ABOMINATIONS OF THE EARTH.**" The KJV bible Greek Strong's Concordance word for "**MYSTERY**" is #**3466** and is the word **μυστήριον mystērion** which means a hidden or secret thing, not obvious to the understanding. The KJV bible Greek Strong's Concordance word for "HARLOTS" is#**4204** and is the word **πόρνη pornē** which means a prostitute, a harlot, an idolater, one who yields themselves to defilement for the sake of gain."

138

THE DEVIL IS LUST, LIES, AND DELUSIONS; AND
THE MOST IS LOVE AND TRUTH WITHOUT CONFUSION!

CHILDREN OF THE MOST HIGH:
PRISTINE YOUTH AND FAMILY SOLUTIONS, LLC.
SONS AND DAUGHTERS OF THE MOST HIGH PUBLISHERS ®

OH, GRACIOUS MOST HIGH HEAVENLY FATHER, HOLY IS YOUR
NAME, YOUR WILL BE DONE NOW AND FOREVER!

Porne is the etymological root word for "**Pornography**" which the Online American Heritage Dictionary (2020) defines as: "**Sexually explicit writing, images, video, or other material whose primary purpose is to cause sexual arousal. Lurid or sensational material.** Often used in combination: **violence pornography. [French pornographie, from pornographe, pornographer, from Late Greek pornographos, writing about prostitutes: porne̅, prostitute**; see per-5 in the Appendix of Indo-European roots + graphein, to write; see -**GRAPHY.**" So, the **MYSTERY name of the Harlot** in the KJV bible book of Revelation chapter 17 that gave birth to the **Global Devil's Web Pharmacy Garden of Poison Seeds is** "**Porne**" or **Pornography.** "**Porne**" is rooted in "**Lusts**", which is **the 3rd of the 9 Deadly Venoms of Desires of the great dragon, that old serpent called the devil and satan** (Hughes, 2019).

139

CHILDREN OF THE MOST HIGH:
PRISTINE YOUTH AND FAMILY SOLUTIONS, LLC.
SONS AND DAUGHTERS OF THE MOST HIGH PUBLISHERS ®

Which is what the Messiah Yashu'a (Jesus) warned us about in the KJV bible book of John chapter 8:44; where he said to the Jews of his day and time: "Ye are of your father the devil, and the **lusts** of your father ye will do. **He** was a murderer from the beginning, and abode not in the truth, because there is no truth in **him**. When **he** speaketh a lie, **he** speaketh of **his** own: for **he** is a liar, and the father of it." Also, the words, **he**, **him** and **his** refers to **one individual** (phonetically is: **in-the-visual** or "I want to be seen or **in-the-visual** (**individual**) feeling of Power**") which denotes the "**I**" principle which grows in **Devil's Web Pharmacy Garden of Poison Seeds**, and it is rooted in "**Pride**", which is the **1st** of The 9 Deadly Venoms of Desires of the great dragon, that old serpent called the devil and satan. When a person is in position of power in society, it does not change a person, it publicly reveals who the person who sits in the seat of power really is.

CHILDREN OF THE MOST HIGH:
PRISTINE YOUTH AND FAMILY SOLUTIONS, LLC.
SONS AND DAUGHTERS OF THE MOST HIGH PUBLISHERS ®

OH, GRACIOUS MOST HIGH HEAVENLY FATHER, HOLY IS YOUR
NAME, YOUR WILL BE DONE NOW AND FOREVER!

Universal Love is against Individuality, which is why the
word "**Universe**" consists of the two syllables of "**Uni**" **(One)**
Verse (Against) or "**ALL**" or "**The ALL**" is against
"**Individuality.**" "**Pride**", and **the Me, Myself** and **I Trinity**
are the children of the "EGO", the KJV bible Greek Strong's
Concordance#1473 word: **ἐγώ egō** which means: **I, me, my**; a
primary pronoun of the first person "**I**" and are the greatest
barriers to experiencing the Most High Heavenly Father
through obedience to the "**Will**" and "**Commandments**" of
Most High. Remember: it was the "**EGO**" of the great dragon,
that old serpent called the devil and satan that filled his chest
with "**Pride**", and he got very hot with great wrath (when a
person gets very angry, their body temperature rises and their
personality can change from positive to negative) before him
and his angels (messengers) got into a war with the Arch
Angelic-Being **Miykaa'el (Michael)** and his **Malaaikat**
(Angels/Messengers) in the KJV bible book of Revelation
chapter 12 verses 7-12.

141

CHILDREN OF THE MOST HIGH:
PRISTINE YOUTH AND FAMILY SOLUTIONS, LLC.
SONS AND DAUGHTERS OF THE MOST HIGH PUBLISHERS ®

OH, GRACIOUS MOST HIGH HEAVENLY FATHER, HOLY IS YOUR
NAME, YOUR WILL BE DONE NOW AND FOREVER!

That's why the KJV bible book of Proverbs chapter 16 verse 18; states: "**Pride goeth before destruction**, **and a haughty spirit before a fall**." The KJV bible Hebrew Strong's Concordance "**#1363** for the word phrase "**and a haughty**" is גֹּבַהּ **gobahh** and means: **arrogance, boastful, pouting out of anger**, and **full of pride**."

CHILDREN OF THE MOST HIGH:
PRISTINE YOUTH AND FAMILY SOLUTIONS, LLC.
SONS AND DAUGHTERS OF THE MOST HIGH PUBLISHERS ®

OH, GRACIOUS MOST HIGH HEAVENLY FATHER, HOLY IS YOUR
NAME, YOUR WILL BE DONE NOW AND FOREVER!

"And I heard a loud voice saying in heaven, Now is come salvation, and strength, and the kingdom of our God, and the power of his Christ: for the accuser of our brethren is cast down, which accused them before our God day and night. And they overcame him by the blood of the Lamb, and by the word of their testimony; and they loved not their lives unto the death. Therefore rejoice, ye heavens, and ye that dwell in them. **Woe to the inhabitants of the earth and of the sea! for the devil is come down unto you, having great wrath, because he knoweth that he hath but a short time, KJV Revelation 12:10-12**."

The Sword of the Spirit
is the Word of God
Ephesian 6:17
The Word of God is Alive and Active,
Sharper than any Double Edged Sword,
It cuts all the way through,
to where joints and marrows come together,
It Judges the desires and thoughts of the heart
Hebrews 4:12

143

THE DEVIL IS LUST, LIES, AND DELUSIONS; AND
THE MOST IS LOVE AND TRUTH WITHOUT CONFUSION!

CHILDREN OF THE MOST HIGH:
PRISTINE YOUTH AND FAMILY SOLUTIONS, LLC.
SONS AND DAUGHTERS OF THE MOST HIGH PUBLISHERS ®

OH, GRACIOUS MOST HIGH HEAVENLY FATHER, HOLY IS YOUR
NAME, YOUR WILL BE DONE NOW AND FOREVER!

So, as it relates to being an obedient child of the Most High, Pride (**P**), Porne or Pornography (**P**) and the "**I**" **principle** grows the "**I**" **want to be seen or in-the-visual (individual)** feeling of Power (**P**) are all from the 9 Venoms of the great dragon which is revealed in the **3 PPPs'** being turned upside down as the numbers **666**. In the KJV bible book of **Revelation chapter 13 verse 18**; it states: "**Here is wisdom. Let him that hath understanding count the number of the beast: for it is the number of a man** (the KJV bible Greek **Strong's Concordance#444 for the word "man" is ἄνθρωπος anthrōpos and means a person or human being, whether male or female); and his (or her or their) number is Six hundred threescore and six (666).**"

In the KJV bible book of **Isaiah chapter 14 verse 16**; it states: "They that see thee shall narrowly look upon thee, and consider thee, saying, is this the **man** that made the earth to tremble, that did shake kingdoms."

THE DEVIL IS LUST, LIES, AND DELUSIONS; AND THE MOST IS LOVE AND TRUTH WITHOUT CONFUSION!

CHILDREN OF THE MOST HIGH:
PRISTINE YOUTH AND FAMILY SOLUTIONS, LLC.
SONS AND DAUGHTERS OF THE MOST HIGH PUBLISHERS ®

OH, GRACIOUS MOST HIGH HEAVENLY FATHER, HOLY IS YOUR NAME, YOUR WILL BE DONE NOW AND FOREVER!

145

CHILDREN OF THE MOST HIGH:
PRISTINE YOUTH AND FAMILY SOLUTIONS, LLC.
SONS AND DAUGHTERS OF THE MOST HIGH PUBLISHERS ®

In the KJV bible book of **Ezekiel 28 verses 1-10**; it states: "The word of the Lord came again unto me, saying, Son of man, say unto the prince of Tyrus, Thus saith the Lord God; Because thine heart is lifted up, and thou hast said, I am a God, I sit in the seat of God, in the midst of the seas; yet thou art a man, and not God, though thou set thine heart as the heart of God. Behold, thou art wiser than Daniel; there is no secret that they can hide from thee. With thy wisdom and with thine understanding thou hast gotten thee riches, and hast gotten gold and silver into thy treasures. By thy great wisdom and by thy traffic hast thou increased thy riches, and thine heart is lifted up because of thy riches. Therefore, thus saith the Lord God; Because thou hast set thine heart as the heart of God. Behold, therefore I will bring strangers upon thee, the terrible of the nations: and they shall draw their swords against the beauty of thy wisdom, and they shall defile thy **brightness**."

146

CHILDREN OF THE MOST HIGH:
PRISTINE YOUTH AND FAMILY SOLUTIONS, LLC.
SONS AND DAUGHTERS OF THE MOST HIGH PUBLISHERS ®

OH, GRACIOUS MOST HIGH HEAVENLY FATHER, HOLY IS YOUR
NAME, YOUR WILL BE DONE NOW AND FOREVER!

"They shall bring thee down to the pit, and thou shalt die the deaths of them that are slain in the midst of the seas. **Wilt thou yet say before him that slayeth thee, I am God? but thou shalt be a man, and no God, in the hand of him that slayeth thee**. Thou shalt die the deaths of the uncircumcised by the hand of strangers: for I have spoken it, saith the Lord God."

It is not possible to be an obedient child of the Most High without surrendering the "I" **principle and converting the "EGO" into the eternal obedient service to the "Will" of the Most High Heavenly Father. By surrendering the "I" principle**, over time with a lot of personal hard work on yourself, a person may become free from all of the 9 Deadly Venoms of the Desires of the great dragon, that old serpent called the devil and satan.

147

CHILDREN OF THE MOST HIGH:
PRISTINE YOUTH AND FAMILY SOLUTIONS, LLC.
SONS AND DAUGHTERS OF THE MOST HIGH PUBLISHERS ®

OH, GRACIOUS MOST HIGH HEAVENLY FATHER, HOLY IS YOUR NAME, YOUR WILL BE DONE NOW AND FOREVER!

In the KJV bible book of Revelation chapter 18 verses 1, 2, 13 and 23 states: "And after these things I saw another angel come down from heaven, having great power; and the earth was lightened with his glory. And he cried mightily with a strong voice, saying, Babylon the great is fallen, is fallen, and is become the habitation of **devils**, and the hold of every foul spirit, and a cage of every unclean and hateful bird." And cinnamon, and odours, and ointments, and frankincense, and wine, and oil, and fine flour, and wheat, and beasts, and sheep, and horses, and chariots, and slaves, and souls of men. And the light of a candle shall shine no more at all in thee; and the voice of the bridegroom and of the bride shall be heard no more at all in thee: for thy merchants were the great men of the earth; for by thy **sorceries** were all nations deceived."

CHILDREN OF THE MOST HIGH:
PRISTINE YOUTH AND FAMILY SOLUTIONS, LLC.
SONS AND DAUGHTERS OF THE MOST HIGH PUBLISHERS ®

OH, GRACIOUS MOST HIGH HEAVENLY FATHER, HOLY IS YOUR
NAME, YOUR WILL BE DONE NOW AND FOREVER!

In the KJV bible book of Revelation chapter 18 verse 23; the word for "**sorceries**" is the KJV bible Greek **Strong's Concordance#5331word**: φαρμακεία **pharmakeia** which is the original Greek root word of where the word "**Pharmacy** and **Pharmaceuticals**" originates from. In the KJV bible book of Galatians chapter 5 verses 19-21; it states: "Now the works of the flesh are manifest, which are these; adultery, fornication, uncleanness, lasciviousness, Idolatry, **witchcraft**, hatred, variance, emulations, wrath, strife, seditions, heresies, envyings, murders, drunkenness, reveling, and such like: of the which I tell you before, as I have also told you in time past, that they which do such things shall not inherit the kingdom of God."

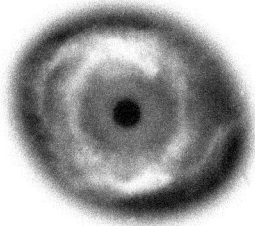

149

CHILDREN OF THE MOST HIGH:
PRISTINE YOUTH AND FAMILY SOLUTIONS, LLC.
SONS AND DAUGHTERS OF THE MOST HIGH PUBLISHERS ®

OH, GRACIOUS MOST HIGH HEAVENLY FATHER, HOLY IS YOUR
NAME, YOUR WILL BE DONE NOW AND FOREVER!

In the KJV bible book of Galatians chapter 5 verse 20; the word for "**witchcraft**" **is the KJV bible Greek Strong's Concordance "#5331word: φαρμακεία pharmakeia which is the original Greek root word of where the word "Pharmacy and Pharmaceuticals" originates from**." The Pharmaceutical companies make opioids and pain medication that many people have become addicted to which grows the opioids "addiction" crisis in America.

150

THE DEVIL IS LUST, LIES, AND DELUSIONS; AND
THE MOST IS LOVE AND TRUTH WITHOUT CONFUSION!

CHILDREN OF THE MOST HIGH:
PRISTINE YOUTH AND FAMILY SOLUTIONS, LLC.
SONS AND DAUGHTERS OF THE MOST HIGH PUBLISHERS ®

OH, GRACIOUS MOST HIGH HEAVENLY FATHER, HOLY IS YOUR
NAME, YOUR WILL BE DONE NOW AND FOREVER!

However, in fairness, many people have taken opioids as prescribed by their medical physicians and did not become addicted to opioids. Opioids "**addiction**" adds to preexisting addictions such as tobacco, alcohol, illegal and legal substance abuse addictions which continues to grow the number of people who become addicted to pharmaceutical drugs and become addicts amongst members of humanity. **Leviathan, as a sex force, utilizes Porne to grow "Lusts", the 3rd of the 9 Deadly Venoms of Desires of the great dragon, that old serpent called the devil and satan in the global Devil's Web Pharmacy Garden of Poison Seeds.** For more information about the 9 Deadly Venoms of Desires of the great dragon, that old serpent called the devil and satan, refer to the book entitled: **"Spiritual Trillionaire: Cherishing the Breath of Life While Simultaneously Preparing for the Blow of Death,"** Hughes, 2019."

151

CHILDREN OF THE MOST HIGH:
PRISTINE YOUTH AND FAMILY SOLUTIONS, LLC.
SONS AND DAUGHTERS OF THE MOST HIGH PUBLISHERS ®

OH, GRACIOUS MOST HIGH HEAVENLY FATHER, HOLY IS YOUR
NAME, YOUR WILL BE DONE NOW AND FOREVER!

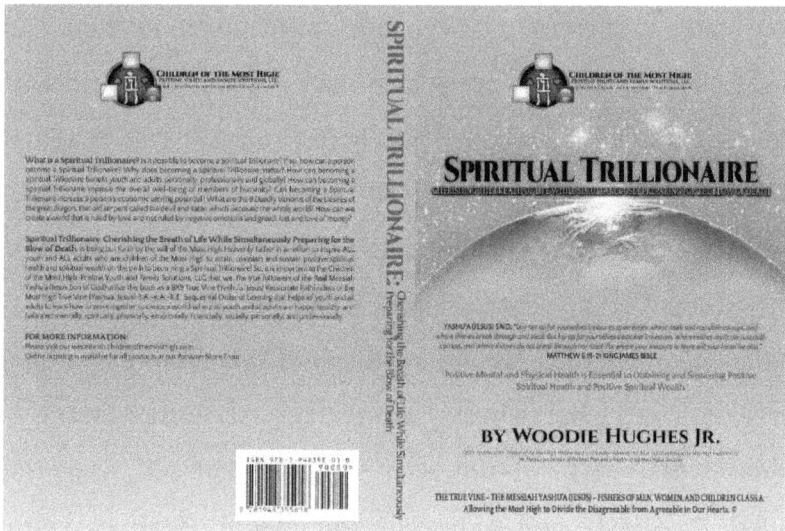

In the KJV bible book of Leviticus chapter 19 verse 31; it states: "Regard **not them that have familiar spirits**, neither seek after **wizards** "to be defiled by them: I [am] the LORD your God." In the KJV bible book of Leviticus chapter 20 verse 6; it states: "And the soul that turneth after **such as have familiar spirits**, and after **wizards**, to go a whoring after them, I will even set my face against that soul, and will cut him off from among his people."

152

THE DEVIL IS LUST, LIES, AND DELUSIONS; AND
THE MOST IS LOVE AND TRUTH WITHOUT CONFUSION!

CHILDREN OF THE MOST HIGH:
PRISTINE YOUTH AND FAMILY SOLUTIONS, LLC.
SONS AND DAUGHTERS OF THE MOST HIGH PUBLISHERS ®

OH, GRACIOUS MOST HIGH HEAVENLY FATHER, HOLY IS YOUR
NAME, YOUR WILL BE DONE NOW AND FOREVER!

"In the KJV bible book of Leviticus chapter 19 verse 31, and Leviticus chapter 20 verse 6; the word for "**wizards**" is the **KJV bible Hebrew Strong's Concordance#3045 word**: "**Yiddehone**e" יִדְּעֹנִי yidd@`oniy which means **soothsayer, necromancer, a knowing one; specifically, a conjurer; (by implication) a ghost; wizard.**"

יִדְעֹנִי m. pl. יִדְּעֹנִים.—(1) properly knowing, wise, hence *a prophet, a wizard*, always used in a bad sense of false prophets. Lev. 19:31; 20:6; Deut. 18:11; 1 Sa. 28:3, 9 (comp. عَالِم prop. knowing, a magician, like the Germ. weiſer Mann, kluge Frau, used of wizards uttering words to the deluded people.)

(2) *a spirit of divination, a spirit of python* with which these soothsayers were believed to be in communication. Lev. 20:27; comp. אוֹב.

153

CHILDREN OF THE MOST HIGH:
PRISTINE YOUTH AND FAMILY SOLUTIONS, LLC.
SONS AND DAUGHTERS OF THE MOST HIGH PUBLISHERS ®

OH, GRACIOUS MOST HIGH HEAVENLY FATHER, HOLY IS YOUR
NAME, YOUR WILL BE DONE NOW AND FOREVER!

In the aforementioned KJV bible book of Leviticus chapter 19 verse 31, and Leviticus chapter 20 verse 6; the word for phrases "<u>**not them that have familiar spirits**</u> and <u>**such as have familiar spirits**</u>" is the **KJV bible Hebrew Strong's Concordance#178 word: אוב 'owb which means ghost, spirit of a dead one**. So, in summary, the aforementioned information explains the correlation between what the bible refers to as <u>**sorcery**</u>, <u>**witchcraft, familiar spirits and the Mystery name of the Harlot who gave birth to the Global Devil's Web Pharmacy Garden of Poison Seed**</u>s as it relates to a person being on the path to becoming one of the obedient children of the Most High. It also clarifies why **God (Elohiym) is against the children of the Most High utilizing or experimenting with Ouija boards or spirit boards, porne, soothsayers, necromancers, sorceries, witchcraft, familiar spirits and overcoming the "I" principle.**

154

CHILDREN OF THE MOST HIGH:
PRISTINE YOUTH AND FAMILY SOLUTIONS, LLC.
SONS AND DAUGHTERS OF THE MOST HIGH PUBLISHERS ®

OH, GRACIOUS MOST HIGH HEAVENLY FATHER, HOLY IS YOUR
NAME, YOUR WILL BE DONE NOW AND FOREVER!

So, it is crucial for all children of the Most High to have or create **Predetermined S.M.A.R.T.** **(Single-Minded, Achievable, Reasonable, Timed) Goals** for themselves to intentionally not waste time, but rather maximize the utilization of time wisely at all time! Being an obedient child of the Most High requires a person to rigorously commit themselves with a sincere and compassionate heart to the service of the Most High Heavenly Father ONLY! Service is the vehicle by which the children of the Most High travels in life. Love is the zeal and speed of the vehicle by which the children of the Most High travels in life, and wisdom is the way that the children of the Most High travels in life. Therefore; knowing the aforementioned is essential for those who don't want to be deceived by the devil's lusts, lies and delusions; but rather acknowledge that the Most High is love and truth without confusion!

CHILDREN OF THE MOST HIGH:
PRISTINE YOUTH AND FAMILY SOLUTIONS, LLC.
SONS AND DAUGHTERS OF THE MOST HIGH PUBLISHERS ®

Chapter 7: Why do You use the Devil's Horns Hand Signs If You Say that you Trust in the Most High and the True Vine (Yashu'a, Jesus)?

Three versions of the "El Diablo (The Devil)," the devil hand signs. The same devil who is referred to in the KJV bible book of Revelation chapter 12 verses 7-9 as "the great dragon, that old serpent called the devil and satan that deceived the whole world" that according to KJV bible book of Isaiah chapter 14 verse 16 is on the planet earth with his fallen angels as <u>a man</u>.

THE DEVIL IS LUST, LIES, AND DELUSIONS; AND
THE MOST IS LOVE AND TRUTH WITHOUT CONFUSION!

CHILDREN OF THE MOST HIGH:
PRISTINE YOUTH AND FAMILY SOLUTIONS, LLC.
SONS AND DAUGHTERS OF THE MOST HIGH PUBLISHERS ®

OH, GRACIOUS MOST HIGH HEAVENLY FATHER, HOLY IS YOUR
NAME, YOUR WILL BE DONE NOW AND FOREVER!

According to a November 9, 2019 "Truth is always Stranger Than Fiction" article entitled: **"Breaking Down the Occult Meaning Of 'El Diablo' Or the Satanic Horns Hand,"**

The article states: "It is being flashed everywhere – on TV, in newspapers and magazines, at sporting events, and even at presidential inaugurations. I'm referring, of course, to the sign of **El Diablo, the horned devil**, also known as the **sign of the horns**."

157

CHILDREN OF THE MOST HIGH:
PRISTINE YOUTH AND FAMILY SOLUTIONS, LLC.
SONS AND DAUGHTERS OF THE MOST HIGH PUBLISHERS ®

**It was popularized in the '60s by the founder of the Church
of Satan, Anton LaVey,** who spread it to the masses through
rock musicians who were deep into satanism. Today, it is a hand
sign for '**rock and roll**'.

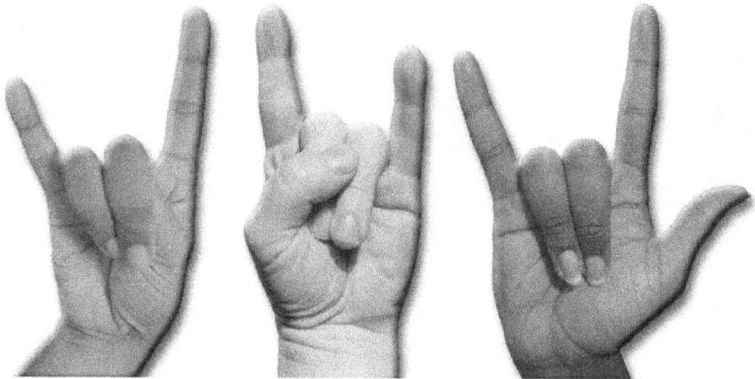

The article also states: "**There are three versions** of the *El
Diablo*, **the horned god or the sign of Satan.** The hand sign at
left with the thumb in is meant to be used for the right hand,
Anton LaVey called it '**The sign of the curse**', while the sign
in the middle is meant for the left hand with thumb in between,

THE DEVIL IS LUST, LIES, AND DELUSIONS; AND
THE MOST IS LOVE AND TRUTH WITHOUT CONFUSION!

CHILDREN OF THE MOST HIGH:
PRISTINE YOUTH AND FAMILY SOLUTIONS, LLC.
SONS AND DAUGHTERS OF THE MOST HIGH PUBLISHERS ®

OH, GRACIOUS MOST HIGH HEAVENLY FATHER, HOLY IS YOUR
NAME, YOUR WILL BE DONE NOW AND FOREVER!

it is usually used to curse someone by pointing it directly towards the person, and at the right is also the '**deaf's gesture**', and the hand sign, for '**I love you**' a fact which has many people confused."

Who is Anton LaVey? According to the **1972 TIME Magazine Article**,

"**Anton LaVey is founder of the <u>Church of Satan in San Francisco in 1966</u>**. But the existence of Satanists as an organized, public group in the United States is a much newer phenomenon, much of which can be largely traced to one man: **Anton Szandor La Vey, author of 1969's The Satanic Bible**."

159

THE DEVIL IS LUST, LIES, AND DELUSIONS; AND
THE MOST IS LOVE AND TRUTH WITHOUT CONFUSION!

CHILDREN OF THE MOST HIGH:
PRISTINE YOUTH AND FAMILY SOLUTIONS, LLC.
SONS AND DAUGHTERS OF THE MOST HIGH PUBLISHERS ®

OH, GRACIOUS MOST HIGH HEAVENLY FATHER, HOLY IS YOUR
NAME, YOUR WILL BE DONE NOW AND FOREVER!

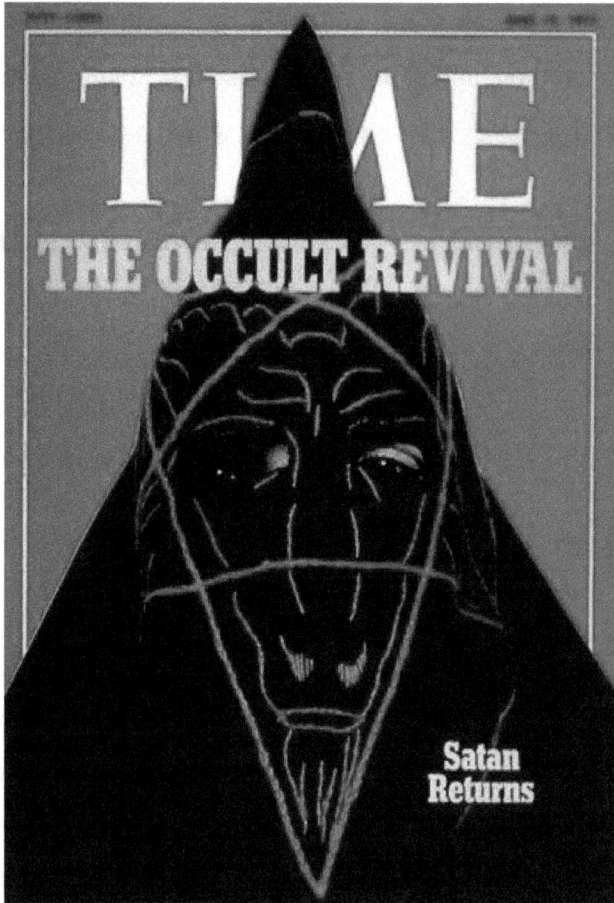

The June 19, 1972, cover of TIME

CHILDREN OF THE MOST HIGH:
PRISTINE YOUTH AND FAMILY SOLUTIONS, LLC.
SONS AND DAUGHTERS OF THE MOST HIGH PUBLISHERS ®

OH, GRACIOUS MOST HIGH HEAVENLY FATHER, HOLY IS YOUR
NAME, YOUR WILL BE DONE NOW AND FOREVER!

Phonetically, what is the reverse of "Levi-athan"?

Phonetically, the reverse of "**Levi-athan**" is "**Anton LaVey**" which spelled backwards as: **LaVey Anton** is phonetically pronounced as: "**Leviathan**". **What does Leviathan mean according to the KJV bible?** According to the bible, "**Levi**" means "**Law**" and "**athan**" means "**sin**". Could **Leviathan** be the law that governed the **serpent in the Garden of Eden** in the KJV bible book of Genesis chapter 3 verse 1? "Now the **serpent (KJV bible Hebrew Strong's Concordance#5175, <u>as</u> נָחָשׁ Nakhash (Nachash) word for "serpent" in the modern Hebrew language. "Nakhash," in the ancient Aramaic language means "Whisperer")** was more subtle than any beast of the field which **the LORD God had made**. And he said unto the woman, Yea, hath God said, Ye shall not eat of every tree of the garden."

161

CHILDREN OF THE MOST HIGH:
PRISTINE YOUTH AND FAMILY SOLUTIONS, LLC.
SONS AND DAUGHTERS OF THE MOST HIGH PUBLISHERS ®

According to Gowan (1988), many theologians, and practitioners of Judaism, Christianity and Islam refer to the **Serpent** in the KJV bible book of Genesis as another title for **"the devil"** or **"satan"** or **"Lucifer"** as mentioned in the KJV bible book of Isaiah chapter 14 verse 12. The KJV bible book of Isaiah chapter 14 verse 12 with Hebrew inserts states:

אֵיךְ נָפַלְתָּ מִשָּׁמַיִם הֵילֵל בֶּן־שָׁחַר נִגְדַּעְתָּ לָאָרֶץ חוֹלֵשׁ
עַל־גּוֹיִם:

"How art thou fallen (נָפַל **Naphal**) from heaven (שָׁמַיִם shamayim) O Lucifer (**Halal; Hallal** הֵילֵל) or (הֵילֵל **Heylel**) son (בֶּן **Ben**) of the morning (שַׁחַר **Shakhar (Shachar)** (יָלַל **Yalal**) how art thou cut down (גָּדַע **Gada`**) to the ground (אֶרֶץ **'Erets**) which didst weaken (**Chalash**) the nations (גּוֹי **Gowy**)."

Hence, **Lucifer** is sometimes referred to as **a serpent**. The pluralization of **Lucifer** is **Luciferians** or is sometimes referred to as **Legions**.

CHILDREN OF THE MOST HIGH:
PRISTINE YOUTH AND FAMILY SOLUTIONS, LLC.
SONS AND DAUGHTERS OF THE MOST HIGH PUBLISHERS ®

In the KJV bible book of Mark chapter 5 verse 9; Yashu'a (Jesus) asked him (**the unclean spirits inside the man that was possessed**): "What [is] thy name? And he answered, saying, **my name [is] Legion: for we are many**." The KJV bible Greek Strong's Concordance "**#3003**, defines: "λεγιών **Legion**" as a body of soldiers whose number differed at different times. The KJV bible Hebrew Strong's Concordance **#03882**, defines: "**Leviathan**" לִוְיָתָן **livyâthân, liv-yaw-thawn'**; **as a sea monster, dragon from Lawwaw meaning: to unite, to remain**. In the KJV bible book of Isaiah chapter 27 verse 1; **Leviathan is literally called the: "piercing <u>serpent</u>"**. The **KJV bible Strong's Hebrew Concordance# 5175**, defines: "**<u>Serpent</u>" as נָחָשׁ Nachash or Nakhash** which is the same word used the KJV bible book of Genesis chapter 3 verse 1, that is being interpreted as "**the devil**"."

163

CHILDREN OF THE MOST HIGH:
PRISTINE YOUTH AND FAMILY SOLUTIONS, LLC.
SONS AND DAUGHTERS OF THE MOST HIGH PUBLISHERS ®

OH, GRACIOUS MOST HIGH HEAVENLY FATHER, HOLY IS YOUR
NAME, YOUR WILL BE DONE NOW AND FOREVER!

In the KJV bible book of Mathew chapter 10 verse 1; the Messiah Yashu'a (Jesus): "called unto him his twelve disciples, he gave them power against <u>unclean</u> spirits, to cast them out, and to heal all manner of sickness and all manner of disease." The word "**unclean**" in this verse is KJV bible Greek Strong's Concordance#169 word: "ἀκάθαρτος **akathartos- meaning: not cleansed, unclean; in a ceremonial sense: that which must be abstained from according to the Levitical law; in a moral sense: unclean in thought and life; impure (ceremonially, morally (lewd-crude and offensive in a sexual way, vulgar, filthy, obscene, pornographic, wicked (evil or morally wrong), indecent) or specially, (demonic): foul, unclean).**" Like poisonous venom! **What is venom**? According to the Online American Heritage Dictionary (2020), **venom is defined as**: 1. A poisonous secretion of an animal, such as a snake, spider, or scorpion, usually transmitted to prey or to attackers by a bite or sting."

164

CHILDREN OF THE MOST HIGH:
PRISTINE YOUTH AND FAMILY SOLUTIONS, LLC.
SONS AND DAUGHTERS OF THE MOST HIGH PUBLISHERS ®

OH, GRACIOUS MOST HIGH HEAVENLY FATHER, HOLY IS YOUR
NAME, YOUR WILL BE DONE NOW AND FOREVER!

In the KJV bible book of Job chapter 41 verse 1: "Canst thou draw out **leviathan** with a hook? or his tongue with a cord which thou lettest down?" In the KJV bible book of Psalms chapter 74 verse 14: "Thou brakest the heads of **leviathan** in pieces, and gavest him to be meat to the people inhabiting the wilderness." In the KJV bible book of Psalms chapter 104 verse 26: "There go the ships: there is that **leviathan**, whom thou hast made to play therein."

In the KJV bible book of Isaiah chapter 27 verse 1: "In that day the LORD with his sore and great and strong sword shall punish leviathan the piercing serpent, even leviathan that crooked serpent; and he shall slay the dragon that is in the sea."

165

CHILDREN OF THE MOST HIGH:
PRISTINE YOUTH AND FAMILY SOLUTIONS, LLC.
SONS AND DAUGHTERS OF THE MOST HIGH PUBLISHERS ☀

OH, GRACIOUS MOST HIGH HEAVENLY FATHER, HOLY IS YOUR
NAME, YOUR WILL BE DONE NOW AND FOREVER!

According to the aforementioned KJV bible verses, **Leviathan, the great dragon is a Legion of unclean spirits also known as the Sex Spirit Force called pórnē, por'-nay πόρνη** and pronounced as: **"Pornay"** that the Messiah Yashu'a (Jesus) spoke about in the KJV bible book of John chapter 8 verse 41 below with Greek inserts. **"ὑμεῖς ποιεῖτε τὰ ἔργα τοῦ πατρὸς ὑμῶν εἶπον οὖν αὐτῷ Ἡμεῖς ἐκ πορνείας οὐ γεγεννήμεθα ἕνα πατέρα ἔχομεν τὸν θεόν** (KJV bible book of John chapter 8 verse 41)." In the KJV bible book of John chapter 8 verses 41; Yashu'a (Jesus) stated: "Ye do the deeds of your father. Then said they to him, we be not born of fornication; we have one Father, even God." In the previous verse, the word **"fornication"** is the **KJV bible Greek Strong's Concordance#4202 πορνεία porneia which is defined as an illicit sexual intercourse, adultery, fornication, homosexuality, lesbianism, intercourse with animals etc."**

166

CHILDREN OF THE MOST HIGH:
PRISTINE YOUTH AND FAMILY SOLUTIONS, LLC.
SONS AND DAUGHTERS OF THE MOST HIGH PUBLISHERS ®

OH, GRACIOUS MOST HIGH HEAVENLY FATHER, HOLY IS YOUR
NAME, YOUR WILL BE DONE NOW AND FOREVER!

"The word "**fornication**" πορνεία **porneia**, is from the root word "**pornay**", KJV bible Greek Strong's Concordance **#4202 πόρνη pórnē, por'-nay**; which means an idolater: **harlot, whore**." Ironically, the word: "**quean**" means: ""young, robust woman," Old English **cwene** "woman," also "female serf, **hussy**, **prostitute**" (as in portcwene "public woman"), from Proto-Germanic *kwenon (source also of Old Saxon quan, Old High German quena, Old Norse kona, Gothic qino "wife, woman"), from PIE root *gwen- "woman." Popular 16c.-17c. in sense "**hussy**." "**Sense of "effeminate homosexual" is recorded from 1935, especially in Australian slang** according to the Online Etymology Dictionary (2020)." So, phonetically, does the words: **cwene, quean,** and **queen** sound different? **No!** So, **Sisters**, do you want to refer to yourselves as a **cwene, quean,** or **queen?** Or; as **Sisters who obey the Most High?** **Why?** Because **Sisters who obey the Most High are "True Sisters"** that are "**Daughters of the Most High!**"

167

CHILDREN OF THE MOST HIGH:
PRISTINE YOUTH AND FAMILY SOLUTIONS, LLC.
SONS AND DAUGHTERS OF THE MOST HIGH PUBLISHERS ®

OH, GRACIOUS MOST HIGH HEAVENLY FATHER, HOLY IS YOUR
NAME, YOUR WILL BE DONE NOW AND FOREVER!

The KJV bible book of John chapter 8 verses 44 with Greek inserts: "ὑμεῖς ἐκ πατρὸς τοῦ διαβόλου ἐστὲ καὶ τὰς ἐπιθυμίας τοῦ πατρὸς ὑμῶν θέλετε ποιεῖν ἐκεῖνος ἀνθρωποκτόνος ἦν ἀπ᾽ ἀρχῆς καὶ ἐν τῇ ἀληθείᾳ οὐχ ἔστηκεν ὅτι οὐκ ἔστιν ἀλήθεια ἐν αὐτῷ ὅταν λαλῇ τὸ ψεῦδος ἐκ τῶν ἰδίων λαλεῖ ὅτι ψεύστης ἐστὶν καὶ ὁ πατὴρ αὐτοῦ." In the KJV bible book of John chapter 8 verses 44; Yashu'a (Jesus) stated: "Ye are of your father the devil, and the lusts of your father ye will do. He was a murderer from the beginning, and abode not in the truth, because there is no truth in him. When he speaketh a lie, he speaketh of his own: for he is a liar, and the father of it."

CHILDREN OF THE MOST HIGH:
PRISTINE YOUTH AND FAMILY SOLUTIONS, LLC.
SONS AND DAUGHTERS OF THE MOST HIGH PUBLISHERS ®

OH, GRACIOUS MOST HIGH HEAVENLY FATHER, HOLY IS YOUR
NAME, YOUR WILL BE DONE NOW AND FOREVER!

In the aforementioned verse, the word "**lusts**" is the KJV bible Greek Strong's Concordance "**#1939** word: ἐπιθυμία **epithymia**, which means: **desire, craving, longing, desire for what is forbidden, lust**."

169

CHILDREN OF THE MOST HIGH:
PRISTINE YOUTH AND FAMILY SOLUTIONS, LLC.
SONS AND DAUGHTERS OF THE MOST HIGH PUBLISHERS ®

OH, GRACIOUS MOST HIGH HEAVENLY FATHER, HOLY IS YOUR
NAME, YOUR WILL BE DONE NOW AND FOREVER!

Is there a simple social media message that you can share that will help me to clearly differentiate between love and lust?

Love verse Lust

Love gives	Lust uses
Love is personal	Lust is objectifying
Love is honest	Lust is devious
Love waits	Lust takes
Love is life-giving	Lust is lifeless
Love is life-long	Lust is temporary
Love chooses	Lust uses
Love sympathizes	Lust criticizes
Love is committed	Lust is unattached
Love is faithful	Lust is disloyal
Love is generous	Lust is selfish
Love communicates	Lust manipulates
Love is deep	Lust is shallow
Love is responsive	Lust is insensitive
Love is pure	Lust is impure
Love understands	Lust makes demands
Love is kind	Lust is blind
Love appreciates	Lust intimidates
Love cares	Lust dares
Love accepts	Lust discards
Love is given	Lust is obsessed
Love talks	Lust walks
Love adores	Lust keeps score

www.facebook.com/loveiscourtship

CHILDREN OF THE MOST HIGH:
PRISTINE YOUTH AND FAMILY SOLUTIONS, LLC.
SONS AND DAUGHTERS OF THE MOST HIGH PUBLISHERS ®

OH, GRACIOUS MOST HIGH HEAVENLY FATHER, HOLY IS YOUR
NAME, YOUR WILL BE DONE NOW AND FOREVER!

So far, the KJV bible has established that **Leviathan, the great dragon** is a **Legion (a body of soldiers or many unclean spiritual soldiers that can invade a body)** also known as the **Sex Spirit Force called pórnē, por'-nay πόρνη** and pronounced as: **"Pornay"** that the Messiah Yashu'a (Jesus) spoke about in the KJV bible book of John chapter 8 verses 41-44. The bible also teaches us that this **Lucifer** who leads this **Legion of Luciferians, that old serpent (Leviathan)** who also lived during the time in the KJV bible book of Genesis chapter 3 verse 1 who is being interpreted as the **Devil (and devil spelled backwards is the word: "lived")**. So, this **devil and his angels convey messages to humanity to influence humanity through the Deadly Venom of the Desire of "Lust" as the Sex Spirit Force called Pornay. This old dragon, was called the devil and satan.** So, Lucifer controls a Legion of Leviathans or Luciferians and is also the leader as Satan over a Legion called Satanists.

171

THE DEVIL IS LUST, LIES, AND DELUSIONS; AND THE MOST IS LOVE AND TRUTH WITHOUT CONFUSION!

CHILDREN OF THE MOST HIGH:
PRISTINE YOUTH AND FAMILY SOLUTIONS, LLC.
SONS AND DAUGHTERS OF THE MOST HIGH PUBLISHERS ®

OH, GRACIOUS MOST HIGH HEAVENLY FATHER, HOLY IS YOUR NAME, YOUR WILL BE DONE NOW AND FOREVER!

Therefore, it is essential for the children of the Most High to guard themselves against the Luciferians and Satanists by being obedient the Most High Heavenly Father! By doing so, a person learns to utilize the bible as a tool against the devil's lusts, lies and delusions by studying the KJV bible Hebrew and Greek Strong's Concordance hidden meanings of the etymology of the English translated words or the translated words of any other language that their scriptures were translated into. By researching the original root meanings of the original languages that the scriptures were revealed in, it affords a person an opportunity to acquire the original messages that **Michael and his angels** according the KJV bible book of Revelation chapter 12, conveys to members of humanity. Thus, affording one to learn that the Satanists seek mind control and dominance and the Luciferians seek to control the energy of others.

172

CHILDREN OF THE MOST HIGH:
PRISTINE YOUTH AND FAMILY SOLUTIONS, LLC.
SONS AND DAUGHTERS OF THE MOST HIGH PUBLISHERS ®

OH, GRACIOUS MOST HIGH HEAVENLY FATHER, HOLY IS YOUR
NAME, YOUR WILL BE DONE NOW AND FOREVER!

They are best described as: Spiritual Vampires!

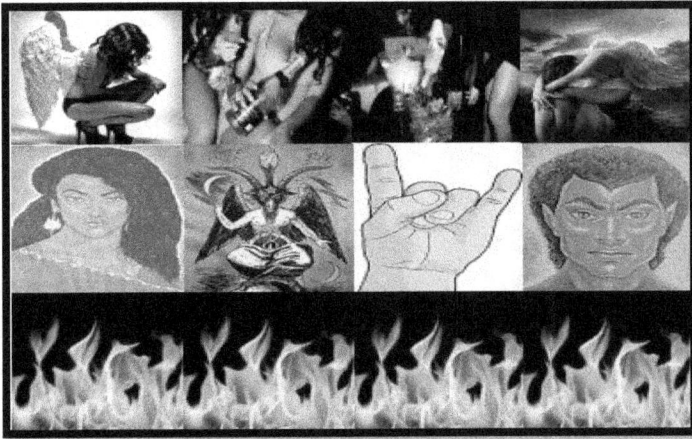

Spiritual Vampires are beings who draw energy from others which also can occur to a person who is striving to be positive while listening to negative speaking people or a negative speaking person. Therefore; the aforementioned is for the children of the Most High to beware of and to put into moment to moment action to best be able to prevent being deceived by the devil's lust, lies and delusions while simultaneously being empowered, inspired, and guided from moment to moment by the Most High's love and truth without confusion!

173

CHILDREN OF THE MOST HIGH:
PRISTINE YOUTH AND FAMILY SOLUTIONS, LLC.
SONS AND DAUGHTERS OF THE MOST HIGH PUBLISHERS ®

OH, GRACIOUS MOST HIGH HEAVENLY FATHER, HOLY IS YOUR
NAME, YOUR WILL BE DONE NOW AND FOREVER!

Chapter 8: Jab, Body Blow, TKO;
Life is More Precious than ALL of the Physical Pleasures
that can hurt you more than you May Know!

"Love not the world, neither the things that are in the world.
If any man [any male or female human being - ἄνθρωπος
anthrōpos] love the world, the love of the Father is not in
him. For all that is in the world, the lust of the flesh, and the
lust of the eyes, and the pride of life, is not of the Father, but
is of the world. And the world passeth away, and the lust
thereof: but he that doeth the will of God abideth forever,
KJV bible book of 1 John chapter 2 verses: 15-17)."

174

CHILDREN OF THE MOST HIGH:
PRISTINE YOUTH AND FAMILY SOLUTIONS, LLC.
SONS AND DAUGHTERS OF THE MOST HIGH PUBLISHERS ®

OH, GRACIOUS MOST HIGH HEAVENLY FATHER, HOLY IS YOUR
NAME, YOUR WILL BE DONE NOW AND FOREVER!

There are 3 types of people in this world:

1. Those who make things happen.

2. Those who watch things happen.

3. Those who wondered what happened.

Which one of the aforementioned types of people best describes you? Everything that taste good is not healthy to eat. Everything that sounds good is not good to listen to. Everything that smells good is not good to inhale. Everything that feels good is not healthy or wise to touch. The body is fictitious play of illusions and ignorance. Attachment to it is bondage. Desires of this world, lead us down the wide road of our own self-destruction. Good health is true wealth! Why do so many people continue to live an unhealthy lifestyle? **Habits**!!!

175

THE DEVIL IS LUST, LIES, AND DELUSIONS; AND
THE MOST IS LOVE AND TRUTH WITHOUT CONFUSION!

CHILDREN OF THE MOST HIGH:
PRISTINE YOUTH AND FAMILY SOLUTIONS, LLC.
SONS AND DAUGHTERS OF THE MOST HIGH PUBLISHERS ®

OH, GRACIOUS MOST HIGH HEAVENLY FATHER, HOLY IS YOUR
NAME, YOUR WILL BE DONE NOW AND FOREVER!

Many people, who do not achieve their goals, engage in habits that prevent them from doing so. Living a healthy lifestyle must become a new habit of passion for the children of the Most High. That passion must become a predetermined purpose, and that purpose must become a mission to be healthy and to stay healthy by: obeying our Most High Heavenly Father, by guarding our minds and hearts, and by taking great care of our overall mental, physical, spiritual, emotional, and financial well-being! However; please know that this is easier said than done for a multitude of diverse reasons, and because many situations that we cannot control, occur in our lives in a twinkling of the eye time (meaning: **in moments, or in less than a moment time**). We can react or respond to life crisis situations, and we can learn to adapt and overcome them, or not adapt to life crisis situations that may overcome us! The blessings are in having the opportunity to learn how to successfully work through the issues and responsibilities that we are obligated to do.

176

CHILDREN OF THE MOST HIGH:
PRISTINE YOUTH AND FAMILY SOLUTIONS, LLC.
SONS AND DAUGHTERS OF THE MOST HIGH PUBLISHERS ®

OH, GRACIOUS MOST HIGH HEAVENLY FATHER, HOLY IS YOUR
NAME, YOUR WILL BE DONE NOW AND FOREVER!

This occurs by us responsibly, fulfilling our agreeable preordained purpose that the Most High Heavenly Father commands of us as children of Most High! Or, we can be like **Everybody**, **Somebody**, **Anybody** and **Nobody** in the story below.

THAT'S NOT MY JOB!

This is a story about four people named: **Everybody, Somebody, Anybody** and **Nobody**. There was an important job to be done and **Everybody** was sure that **Somebody** would do it. **Anybody** could have done it, but **Nobody** did it. **Somebody** got angry about that, because it was **Everybody's** job. **Everybody** thought **Anybody** could do it, but **Nobody** realised that **Everybody** wouldn't do it. It ended up that **Everybody** blamed **Somebody** when **Nobody** did what **Anybody** could have done.

CHILDREN OF THE MOST HIGH:
PRISTINE YOUTH AND FAMILY SOLUTIONS, LLC.
SONS AND DAUGHTERS OF THE MOST HIGH PUBLISHERS ®

OH, GRACIOUS MOST HIGH HEAVENLY FATHER, HOLY IS YOUR
NAME, YOUR WILL BE DONE NOW AND FOREVER!

In the KJV bible book of Exodus chapter 20 verse 16 states: "Thou shalt not bear false witness (**don't lie**)." In the KJV bible book of John chapter 8 verse 44; the Messiah Yashu'a (Jesus) said to the liars in his day and time: "You are of *your* father the devil, and the lusts of your father ye will do. He was a murderer from the beginning, and abode not in the truth, because there is no truth in him. When he speaketh a lie, he speaketh of his own: for he is a liar, and the father of it." Therefore, lets dispel some common lies that we may have heard growing up in this **C.O.A.L** world. **C.O.A.L.** are the acronyms for **C**ulture **O**f **A**ccepting **L**ies. **For example: The road to hell is not paved by good intentions**. The road to hell **is paved by negative intentions**. **It's not wise or safe to rock a baby in a tree top or on top of a tree.**

178

CHILDREN OF THE MOST HIGH:
PRISTINE YOUTH AND FAMILY SOLUTIONS, LLC.
SONS AND DAUGHTERS OF THE MOST HIGH PUBLISHERS ®

Some say: "**it's more than one way to skin a cat**." **All ways of skinning a cat are forms of animal cruelty**, so we must watch our words because there are people that live in this world that have the potential to take these words literally. So, our words should be true, positive, soft and not hard. **It is not nice to tell someone to: "break a leg"** as a statement to mean "**good luck**" which if someone broke their leg, it would be **unfortunate and unlucky**. <u>As children of the Most High, we don't believe in good luck or bad luck</u>. We accept the blessings from the Most High and we accept that **every person will reap what they sow**. Another **Example: <u>The sun does not rise or set, the earth and planets in the 18 galaxy, revolve around the sun</u>**. So, the weather man or the weather woman is wrong every day when he or she tells us what time the **sun rises (comes up)** and the time the **sun sets (goes down)**. <u>**God would not have said that he created the sun, moon and stars because God knows that the sun is a star and that stars are suns**</u>.

179

CHILDREN OF THE MOST HIGH:
PRISTINE YOUTH AND FAMILY SOLUTIONS, LLC.
SONS AND DAUGHTERS OF THE MOST HIGH PUBLISHERS ®

OH, GRACIOUS MOST HIGH HEAVENLY FATHER, HOLY IS YOUR
NAME, YOUR WILL BE DONE NOW AND FOREVER!

God would not refer to the moon as the lesser light because God knows that **the moon is non-illuminous (it does not produce its own light)**, it only reflects the light of the sun. **So, what people refer to as moon light is in actuality sun light that is reflecting off of the moon.** Just because a person looks like they workout, it does not mean that they do; or that they are healthy because they look like they work out. Or just because a person is overweight, it does not mean that they do not exercise regularly or that they are unhealthy according to their lab work (**medical results from testing a person's blood to determine their level of health**) even though their body is shaped different like the shapes of a **circle** and a **square**. Is the **circle** and the **square** different? **They are shaped different, yet they both equal 360 degrees.** Therefore, this teaches the children of the Most High that shapes create illusions. So, just like the **circle** and the **square look different**, **each person on the outside looks different**, **and just like the content of the circle and square is the same; many members of humanity have more similarities than differences.**

180

CHILDREN OF THE MOST HIGH:
PRISTINE YOUTH AND FAMILY SOLUTIONS, LLC.
SONS AND DAUGHTERS OF THE MOST HIGH PUBLISHERS ®

OH, GRACIOUS MOST HIGH HEAVENLY FATHER, HOLY IS YOUR
NAME, YOUR WILL BE DONE NOW AND FOREVER!

For example: most people want to be **happy**, **healthy** and **safe**. If we as a global race of people on the earth focused more on our similarities rather than our differences, more people on the earth may seek ways to work together to help make the world a safer and healthier place for all members of humanity to benefit from.

The aforementioned is for the children of the Most High to beware of and to put into moment to moment **action in their lives** to best be able to prevent being deceived by the devil's lust, lies and delusions while simultaneously being empowered, inspired, and guided from moment to moment by the Most High's love and truth without confusion!

181

CHILDREN OF THE MOST HIGH:
PRISTINE YOUTH AND FAMILY SOLUTIONS, LLC.
SONS AND DAUGHTERS OF THE MOST HIGH PUBLISHERS ®

OH, GRACIOUS MOST HIGH HEAVENLY FATHER, HOLY IS YOUR
NAME, YOUR WILL BE DONE NOW AND FOREVER!

Chapter 9: You Are Uniquely and Wonderfully made, Create ANEW You and Don't Be Afraid!

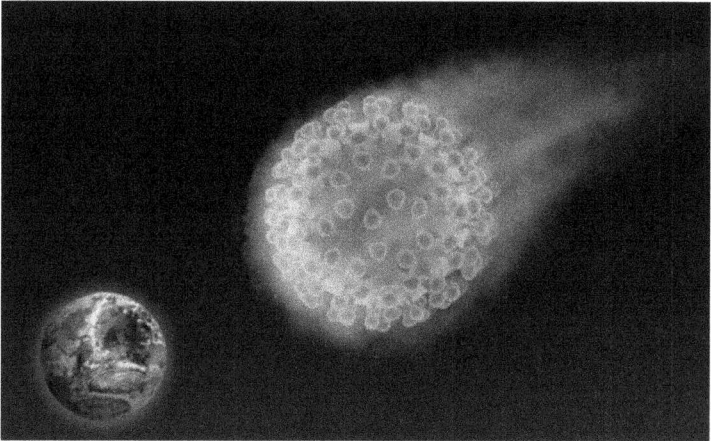

In the KJV bible book of Malachi chapter 4 verses 4-6; it states: "For, behold, the day cometh, that shall burn as an oven; and all the proud, yea, and all that do wickedly, shall be stubble: and the day that cometh shall burn them up, saith the Lord of hosts, that it shall leave them neither root nor branch. Behold, I will send you Elijah the prophet before the coming of the great and dreadful day of the Lord: And he shall turn the heart of the fathers to the children, and the heart of the children to their fathers, lest I come and smite the earth with a curse."

182

CHILDREN OF THE MOST HIGH:
PRISTINE YOUTH AND FAMILY SOLUTIONS, LLC.
SONS AND DAUGHTERS OF THE MOST HIGH PUBLISHERS ®

OH, GRACIOUS MOST HIGH HEAVENLY FATHER, HOLY IS YOUR
NAME, YOUR WILL BE DONE NOW AND FOREVER!

Oh, children of the Most High; be in the world and not of the world! According to the aforementioned KJV bible book of Malachi chapter 4 verses 4-6; a day of reckoning referred to as **"the dreadful day of the Lord"** is coming to the planet earth, to punish wicked people and disobedient people on the planet earth. Is today the day and time of **"the dreadful day of the Lord"? Therefore; it is imperative in this sacred moment in time that the children of the Most High are reminded that NOW is the TIME and Change is the Motive to ensure that our relationship with the Most High and our relationship with ourselves is in order by throughly examining the nature of the content of character of the true reflection of ourselves in the mirror!**

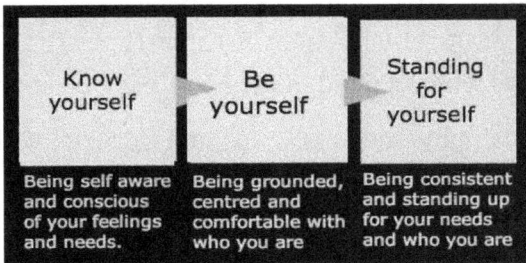

Know yourself	Be yourself	Standing for yourself
Being self aware and conscious of your feelings and needs.	Being grounded, centred and comfortable with who you are	Being consistent and standing up for your needs and who you are

183

CHILDREN OF THE MOST HIGH:
PRISTINE YOUTH AND FAMILY SOLUTIONS, LLC.
SONS AND DAUGHTERS OF THE MOST HIGH PUBLISHERS ®

OH, GRACIOUS MOST HIGH HEAVENLY FATHER, HOLY IS YOUR
NAME, YOUR WILL BE DONE NOW AND FOREVER!

In KJV bible book of John chapter 14 verse 6; Yashu'a (Jesus) said: "I am the way, the truth, and the life: no man cometh unto the Father, but by me."

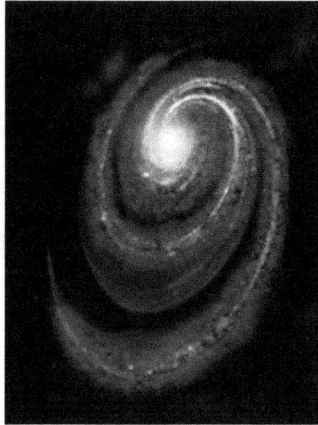

For, the children of the Most High, our inner journey leads to the Most High through the Messiah Yashu'a (Jesus). The starting point is the self, and its' essence is water. Meaning, the starting point is where a child of the Most High experiences the mental, spiritual, physical, emotional and financial willingness to change in the process of becoming devout to the Most High Heavenly Father, now and forever! **Know thyself!**

184

CHILDREN OF THE MOST HIGH:
PRISTINE YOUTH AND FAMILY SOLUTIONS, LLC.
SONS AND DAUGHTERS OF THE MOST HIGH PUBLISHERS *

OH, GRACIOUS MOST HIGH HEAVENLY FATHER, HOLY IS YOUR
NAME, YOUR WILL BE DONE NOW AND FOREVER!

The Children of the Most High: Pristine Youth and Family

Solutions LLC. also utilizes the symbol to represent the portion of the Most High that exists in "**YOU**" and in every person according the KJV bible book of John chapter 1 verses 1-5 and verse 9.

(1). A person's physical body is composed of 70-75% **water.**

(2). The human body is composed of the 99 natural elements on the **earth.**

(3). Human breathing is represented in **wind (oxygen)**.

(4). A person's inner **fire** is referred to as a **solar plexus**.

(5). The totality of a person's entire being is **the (5th) fifth element** as **a creative force of will personified** who utilizes **the 9X9 True Vine (Yashu'a, Jesus) B.A.-K.A.- R.E. Sequential Order of Learning Habits of Success** to help improve every aspect of their life.

185

What keeps a fire burning? Something flammable and oxygen keeps a fire burning. What element does a fire give off? **A fire gives off carbon dioxide**. What do we as human beings breathe in? **We breathe in oxygen**. What do we exhale? **We exhale the element carbon dioxide**. So, there must be something burning inside of each person. When we breathe in **wind (oxygen)** and when blood leaves the heart through the pulmonic valve, into the pulmonary artery and into the lungs, it is oxygenated, it becomes infused or charged like a combustion, **fire**, inside our

hearts 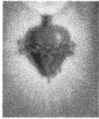 through the "**True Light**" which lighteth every person that comes into the world. In the KJV bible book of John chapter 1 verses 1-5,9; it states: "In the beginning was the Word, and the Word was with God, and the Word was God. The same was in the beginning with God. All things were made by him; and without him was not anything made that was made. In him was life; and the life was the light of men."

186

CHILDREN OF THE MOST HIGH:
PRISTINE YOUTH AND FAMILY SOLUTIONS, LLC.
SONS AND DAUGHTERS OF THE MOST HIGH PUBLISHERS ®

OH, GRACIOUS MOST HIGH HEAVENLY FATHER, HOLY IS YOUR
NAME, YOUR WILL BE DONE NOW AND FOREVER!

"And the light shineth in darkness; and the darkness comprehended it not. [9] That was the true Light, which lighteth every man that cometh into the world."

Air   **Fire**

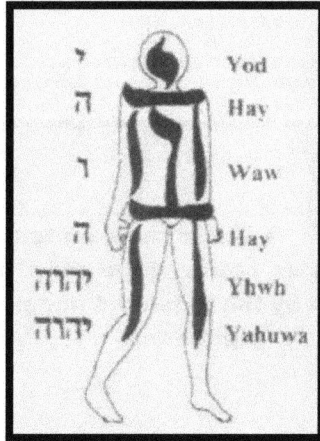

Water   **Earth**

The aforementioned symbol is referred to as the tetragrammaton. **Tetragrammaton is a Greek word** composed of **tetra**-meaning **"four"**, and **gramma**-meaning "**letter**" and has been variously transliterated as **Jhvh, Yhve, Jhwh, Yhwh, Yahayyu, Yahweh, Jehovah, and Yahuwa**.

187

THE DEVIL IS LUST, LIES, AND DELUSIONS; AND
THE MOST IS LOVE AND TRUTH WITHOUT CONFUSION!

CHILDREN OF THE MOST HIGH:
PRISTINE YOUTH AND FAMILY SOLUTIONS, LLC.
SONS AND DAUGHTERS OF THE MOST HIGH PUBLISHERS ®

OH, GRACIOUS MOST HIGH HEAVENLY FATHER, HOLY IS YOUR
NAME, YOUR WILL BE DONE NOW AND FOREVER!

THE FOUR LETTERS ARE:

יהוה YOD IS THE HAND THAT CREATED ALL
HAI IS LIFE
WAW IS THE EYE THAT WATCHES OVER
HAI ALL LIFE

TRANSLATION OF יהוה
O HE WHO IS WHOM HE IS
THE HIDDEN MEANING OF יהוה

WITH HIS HAND HE CREATED ALL
LIFE AND WITH HIS EYE HE WATCHES
OVER ALL LIFE.

YOD also represented all manifested power of the hand. It is symbolized by the extended finger on the right hand.

HAI also represents the breath of life in men, women, and children, and the spirit and soul.

WAW also signifies the ear and is the wind.

188

CHILDREN OF THE MOST HIGH:
PRISTINE YOUTH AND FAMILY SOLUTIONS, LLC.
SONS AND DAUGHTERS OF THE MOST HIGH PUBLISHERS ®

OH, GRACIOUS MOST HIGH HEAVENLY FATHER, HOLY IS YOUR
NAME, YOUR WILL BE DONE NOW AND FOREVER!

Oh, children of the Most High, always remember to be in the world, and not of the world. Meaning, we are physical beings who live in a society that is greatly influenced by the love of the temptations of that which is against the commandments of the Most High. Therefore; it is essential for the children of the Most High to develop the habit of being obedient to the Most High's "**Will**" and commandments rather than giving in to the temptations in a society that is greatly influenced by the love of the temptations that are introduced to us through the **9 Deadly Venoms of the desires of the great dragon, that old serpent, called the devil and satan that deceived the whole world!** Daddy (Mr. Woodie Hughes Sr.) always said: "**Two wrongs, don't make a right!**"

$$Wrong + Wrong \neq Right$$

189

CHILDREN OF THE MOST HIGH:
PRISTINE YOUTH AND FAMILY SOLUTIONS, LLC.
SONS AND DAUGHTERS OF THE MOST HIGH PUBLISHERS ®

OH, GRACIOUS MOST HIGH HEAVENLY FATHER, HOLY IS YOUR
NAME, YOUR WILL BE DONE NOW AND FOREVER!

If you are reading or listening to the words in this book, please do not lose the daily opportunity to increase what you have learned. Nourish your own mental, spiritual, physical and emotional well-being every day before attempting to help others to do the same. In other words, if the vehicle that I am driving is about to run out of gas in the desert, and I receive an emergency call from a close relative or friend who ran out of gas in another part of the same desert; it would be wiser for me to go to the gas station and refill my own vehicle's gas tank first, before going to help a close relative or friend who already ran out of gas. **Daddy (Mr. Woodie Hughes Sr.)** always said: **"You can't push rope, and you can't nail jelly to a wall!"** So, there are many things that we cannot do. However; be aware that the children of the devil are trouble makers that are always working against the children of the Most High who are peacemakers by nature.

190

CHILDREN OF THE MOST HIGH:
PRISTINE YOUTH AND FAMILY SOLUTIONS, LLC.
SONS AND DAUGHTERS OF THE MOST HIGH PUBLISHERS *

OH, GRACIOUS MOST HIGH HEAVENLY FATHER, HOLY IS YOUR
NAME, YOUR WILL BE DONE NOW AND FOREVER!

Therefore; it is to the advantage of children of the Most High to learn and practice the moment to moment mental habit of doing without doing so that all that we are responsible for, gets done. **The act of doing without doing does not mean to not have a strong work ethics, and it does not mean to be lazy and do nothing**. **It means to be at peace while accomplishing the most difficult of tasks and all other tasks every day with maximum effort, skill and efficiency while being in a zone, or only concentrating on the task at hand while in a moment to moment pursuit of becoming and sustaining the willful positive daily habit of being obedient** to our Most High Heavenly Father, now and forever!!! **Positive growth and change requires' rigorous self-introspection, self-reflection and continuous work to practice doing what is necessary for your own overall positive health and well-being; and continued life-long learning every day**!

191

CHILDREN OF THE MOST HIGH:
PRISTINE YOUTH AND FAMILY SOLUTIONS, LLC.
SONS AND DAUGHTERS OF THE MOST HIGH PUBLISHERS ℗

OH, GRACIOUS MOST HIGH HEAVENLY FATHER, HOLY IS YOUR
NAME, YOUR WILL BE DONE NOW AND FOREVER!

During the children of the Most High inner journey experiences, there will be times that nothing that is externally; mentally, physically, spiritually, emotionally and financially distracting will matter when we are overworked or burned out from work or experiencing a stressful life situation, or experiencing a life trauma or society health epidemic or global pandemic. During those times, the renewal of the spirit will matter more than the broken focused due to mental distractions. These are external circumstances that make it more difficult to concentrate and bring in all of our scattered energies (**random unfocused thoughts**) to use those **thoughts (energy)** to renew our minds with intentional positive thinking which is essential to recreating ourselves and essential to balancing our entire being from time to time as needed as a lifelong habit of success! **Oh, children of the Most High,** do your best to think before you speak and act! Practice the moment to moment habit of minimizing avoidable negative adversity by living a lifestyle that does not reflect exhibiting negative behavior!

192

CHILDREN OF THE MOST HIGH:
PRISTINE YOUTH AND FAMILY SOLUTIONS, LLC.
SONS AND DAUGHTERS OF THE MOST HIGH PUBLISHERS ®

OH, GRACIOUS MOST HIGH HEAVENLY FATHER, HOLY IS YOUR
NAME, YOUR WILL BE DONE NOW AND FOREVER!

In other words, avoid the type of conduct that can create **100%
preventable stressful situations in your life and the lives of
others**. Work intentionally and diligently; moment to moment
to be agreeably balanced in the eyesight of the Most High;
nothing in excess! **Oh, children of the Most High,** control the
emotions in you and don't allow the emotions in you to control
you! Exercise patience in all that you are allowed to experience.
**What is patience? Patience is self-control in action over a
period of time, patience is a virtue. What is patience a virtue
of? Patience is a virtue of success!** However; **oh, children of
the Most High; know that we must work diligently and
intentionally to live a lifestyle that reflects us working to
master the three forms of True Vine (Yashu'a, Jesus)
patience! 1. <u>We must exercise patience in obedience to the
Most High</u>. 2. <u>We must exercise patience when experiencing
rebellion within ourselves to do what is best in the eyesight
of the Most High, and when experiencing rebellion from
others</u>.**

193

OH, GRACIOUS MOST HIGH HEAVENLY FATHER, HOLY IS YOUR
NAME, YOUR WILL BE DONE NOW AND FOREVER!

3. <u>We must exercise patience when experiencing misfortune</u>. Seen in its' true light, everything is a test. The <u>reward for patience is patience</u>! Oh, children of the Most High, always remember that the truth about life is that it is hard and dangerous. In the KJV bible book of Matthew chapter 10 verses 26-40; Yashu'a (Jesus) said: "Fear them not therefore: for there is nothing covered, that shall not be revealed; and hid, that shall not be known. What I tell you in darkness, that speak ye in light: and what ye hear in the ear, that preach ye upon the housetops. And fear not them which kill the body, but are not able to kill the soul: but rather fear him which is able to destroy both soul and body in hell. Are not two sparrows sold for a farthing? and one of them shall not fall on the ground without your Father. But the very hairs of your head are all numbered. Fear ye not therefore, ye are of more value than many sparrows. Whosoever therefore shall confess me before men, him will I confess also before my Father which is in heaven."

194

CHILDREN OF THE MOST HIGH:
PRISTINE YOUTH AND FAMILY SOLUTIONS, LLC.
SONS AND DAUGHTERS OF THE MOST HIGH PUBLISHERS ®

OH, GRACIOUS MOST HIGH HEAVENLY FATHER, HOLY IS YOUR
NAME, YOUR WILL BE DONE NOW AND FOREVER!

"But whosoever shall deny me before men, him will I also deny before my Father which is in heaven. "Think not that I am come to send peace on earth: I came not to send peace, but a sword. For I am come to set a man at variance against his father, and the daughter against her mother, and the daughter in law against her mother in law. And a man's foes shall be they of his own household. He that loveth father or mother more than me is not worthy of me: and he that loveth son or daughter more than me is not worthy of me. And he that taketh not his cross, and followeth after me, is not worthy of me. He that findeth his life shall lose it: and he that loseth his life for my sake shall find it. He that receiveth you receiveth me, and he that receiveth me receiveth him that sent me."

You expounded on the devil and his titles in chapter 3; can you expound more on the Devil's nature? In the KJV bible book of Revelation chapter 9 verse 11; it states: "And they had a king over them, which is the angel of the bottomless pit, whose name in the **Hebrew tongue is Abaddon**, but in the **Greek tongue hath his name Apollyon**." In the KJV Hebrew Strong's Concordance "**#11 אבדון Abaddon** means: **destruction**, place of destruction, destruction, **ruin**. In the KJV Greek Strong's Concordance **#623 Ἀπολλύων Apollyōn** means: **Destroyer**! In the KJV bible book of John chapter 8 verse 44; the Messiah Yashu'a (Jesus) said: "Ye are of *your* father the devil, and the <u>lusts</u> of your father ye will do. He was a <u>murderer</u> from the beginning, and abode not in the truth, because there is no truth in him. When he speaketh a lie, he speaketh of his own: for he is a <u>liar</u>, and the father of it." Therefore; according to the aforementioned verses, by nature, the devil is: **the father of ruin**, **father of lusts and lies**, **a murderer**, and **a destroyer**!

196

THE DEVIL IS LUST, LIES, AND DELUSIONS; AND
THE MOST IS LOVE AND TRUTH WITHOUT CONFUSION!

CHILDREN OF THE MOST HIGH:
PRISTINE YOUTH AND FAMILY SOLUTIONS, LLC.
SONS AND DAUGHTERS OF THE MOST HIGH PUBLISHERS ®

OH, GRACIOUS MOST HIGH HEAVENLY FATHER, HOLY IS YOUR
NAME, YOUR WILL BE DONE NOW AND FOREVER!

Is the great dragon, that old serpent, called the devil, and satan attributes of <u>lusts</u>, <u>lies</u> and <u>murdering</u>; the content of the character of those who you refer to as leader, friend, colleague, significant other or person or people who you value? <u>The children of the devil are the children of chaos as their father the devil is the son of perdition</u>. According to the KJV bible book of 2 Timothy chapter 2 verse 3; it states: "Let no man deceive you by any means: for that day shall not come, except there comes a falling away first, and that man of sin be revealed, the **son of perdition**." In the KJV bible Greek Strong's Concordance "**#684**, the phrase: "**of perdition**" is: ἀπώλεια apóleia, ap-o'-li-a; which means: "**destroying, utter destruction of vessels, a perishing, ruin, destruction of money, the destruction which consists of eternal misery in hell, ruin or loss (physical, spiritual or eternal), damnable (nation), destruction, die, perdition, perish, pernicious ways, waste.**"

197

CHILDREN OF THE MOST HIGH:
PRISTINE YOUTH AND FAMILY SOLUTIONS, LLC.
SONS AND DAUGHTERS OF THE MOST HIGH PUBLISHERS ®

OH, GRACIOUS MOST HIGH HEAVENLY FATHER, HOLY IS YOUR
NAME, YOUR WILL BE DONE NOW AND FOREVER!

According to the KJV bible book of 2 Timothy chapter 2 verses 4-10; it states: "Who opposed and exalted himself above all that is called God, or that is worshipped; so that he as God sittest in the temple of God, shewing himself that he is God. Remember ye not, that, when I was yet with you, I told you these things?" "And now ye know what withhold that he might be revealed in his time. For the mystery of iniquity doth already work: only he who now lettest will let, until he be taken out of the way. And then shall that Wicked be revealed, whom the Lord shall consume with the spirit of his mouth, and shall destroy with the brightness of his coming. Even him, who's coming is after the working of Satan with all power and signs and lying wonders, and with all deceivableness of unrighteousness in them that perish; because they received not the love of the truth, that they might be saved. And for this cause, **God shall send them strong delusion, that they should believe a lie**."

198

THE DEVIL IS LUST, LIES, AND DELUSIONS; AND
THE MOST IS LOVE AND TRUTH WITHOUT CONFUSION!

CHILDREN OF THE MOST HIGH:
PRISTINE YOUTH AND FAMILY SOLUTIONS, LLC.
SONS AND DAUGHTERS OF THE MOST HIGH PUBLISHERS ®

OH, GRACIOUS MOST HIGH HEAVENLY FATHER, HOLY IS YOUR
NAME, YOUR WILL BE DONE NOW AND FOREVER!

Since the aforementioned verses highlight some key characteristics about the devil, what are some ways that the children of the Most High can consider before choosing a person or people who pretend to be friends, but are really children of the devil who do not have our best interest at heart? Oh, children of the Most High, guard your mind and guard your heart against all wickedness each moment that you live and exist! Strongly consider not surrounding yourself with people who are in and out of the criminal court due to having a substantiated active criminal history, and a present habit of committing criminal offenses. Guard yourself against words and deeds of deception, and from words that are not true. Consider choosing a friend or friends whose character reflects moral integrity, a friend or friends who actions you have observed over time when things were going well and when they were experiencing adversity.

199

CHILDREN OF THE MOST HIGH:
PRISTINE YOUTH AND FAMILY SOLUTIONS, LLC.
SONS AND DAUGHTERS OF THE MOST HIGH PUBLISHERS ®

OH, GRACIOUS MOST HIGH HEAVENLY FATHER, HOLY IS YOUR
NAME, YOUR WILL BE DONE NOW AND FOREVER!

If your potential friend or friends' positive content of character reflects moral integrity is equal to yours; your friendship will be balanced. Consider choosing a friend or friends who are always seeking to positively improve themselves while simultaneously having a proven positive track record of being a positive influencer, or a mentor, or teacher, or servant-leader in their community, or in their field of expertise, or in any other area that the Most High Heavenly Father has given them the ability to do so. Consider choosing a friend or friends who does not laugh at the thought of you doing something that does not go against the criminal laws of the land that you reside in, and that does not go against the commandments of the Most High! Always remember that people who laugh at those who break the law are not true friends. Consider choosing a friend or friends who seek to achieve excellence in all positive endeavors only, and who encourages you to seek to achieve excellence in all of your positive endeavors. Beware of the argumentative when considering choosing a friend or friends.

200

CHILDREN OF THE MOST HIGH:
PRISTINE YOUTH AND FAMILY SOLUTIONS, LLC.
SONS AND DAUGHTERS OF THE MOST HIGH PUBLISHERS ®

OH, GRACIOUS MOST HIGH HEAVENLY FATHER, HOLY IS YOUR
NAME, YOUR WILL BE DONE NOW AND FOREVER!

<u>Do not argue with the argumentative</u> and <u>do not feed their fire desire to argue with your emotional fuel, and do not ever provoke them with your words!</u> Rather, discipline yourself to not take trivia words, trivia actions, trivia situations, trivia persons, and trivia things personally! <u>**Always remember that the argumentative person or persons who are controlled by their emotions are like a fire that is only hydrated by gasoline!**</u> **Oh, children of the Most High**; consider choosing a friend or friend who avoids all forms of intoxications. **Always remember that the children of the devil always ask: but why? how come? who said so? They often say; "that's not my job."** The children of the devil may not start the majority of conflicts directly; however, they have a habit of making the statements and of asking the questions that lead to conflicts or the perpetuation of existing conflicts that can become barriers to peace.

201

CHILDREN OF THE MOST HIGH:
PRISTINE YOUTH AND FAMILY SOLUTIONS, LLC.
SONS AND DAUGHTERS OF THE MOST HIGH PUBLISHERS ®

OH, GRACIOUS MOST HIGH HEAVENLY FATHER, HOLY IS YOUR NAME, YOUR WILL BE DONE NOW AND FOREVER!

Sometimes, you may hear people say: "There are 3 sides to a story: 1) your side, 2) another person side, and 3) the truth?" However; if a person is standing firm on the Scriptures of the Most High Heavenly Father, and quoting the words of the Most High Heavenly One when teaching or speaking to others; then there are only 2 sides, NOT 3 sides to a story: 1) The Most High Heavenly One's Truth, and 2), The lie or lies in whatever form it may come in of those who conceal the facts of that which they know to be true, or may not know to be true which may lead the sincere-hearted seekers of the Most High Heavenly One's truth astray. So, the aforementioned are some ways that the children of the Most High can consider before choosing a person or people who pretend to be friends, but are really children of the devil who do not have our best interest at heart.

202

CHILDREN OF THE MOST HIGH:
PRISTINE YOUTH AND FAMILY SOLUTIONS, LLC.
SONS AND DAUGHTERS OF THE MOST HIGH PUBLISHERS ✥

OH, GRACIOUS MOST HIGH HEAVENLY FATHER, HOLY IS YOUR
NAME, YOUR WILL BE DONE NOW AND FOREVER!

In the KJV bible book of 1st John chapter 3 verses 9-10; it states: "Whosoever is born of God doth not commit sin; for his **seed** remained in him: and he cannot sin, because he is born of God. In this **the children of God** are manifest, and **the children of the devil:** whosoever doeth not righteousness is not of God, neither he that loveth not his brother." **According to the bible, are people born wicked**? In the KJV bible book of Psalms chapter 58 verses 3-5; it states: "**The wicked are estranged from the womb. The KJV bible Hebrew Strong's Concordance #7358 for the word "estranged" is: רֶחֶם rechem meaning from the womb of a woman**), **they go astray as soon as they be born, speaking lies. Their poison is like the poison of a serpent: they are like the deaf adder that stoppeth her ear; which will not hearken to the voice of charmers, charming never so wisely**." So, according to the aforementioned KJV bible verses, it is now clear who the children of the Most High are, and who the children of the devil are.

203

CHILDREN OF THE MOST HIGH:
PRISTINE YOUTH AND FAMILY SOLUTIONS, LLC.
SONS AND DAUGHTERS OF THE MOST HIGH PUBLISHERS ®

OH, GRACIOUS MOST HIGH HEAVENLY FATHER, HOLY IS YOUR
NAME, YOUR WILL BE DONE NOW AND FOREVER!

In the KJV bible book of Matthew chapter 12 verses 48-50; the Messiah Yashu'a (Jesus) said: "Who is my mother? and who are my brethren? And he stretched forth his hand toward his disciples, and said, behold my mother and my brethren! For whosoever shall do the will of my Father which is in heaven, the same is my brother, and sister, and mother."

What are the biblical signs or characteristics of the wicked children of the devil? The children of the Most High have Divine Love for the Most High ONLY! The children of the Most High also love the Messiah Yashu'a (Jesus). The children of the devil are possessed by the love money rather than loving the Most High Heavenly Father and the Messiah Yashu'a (Jesus). **Why**? Because the children of the devil's hearts are consumed and filled with fear, hate, pride, greed, lusts, lies, and murder, the same as their father the devil; this makes them incapable of loving the Most High Heavenly Father and the Messiah Yashu'a (Jesus).

204

CHILDREN OF THE MOST HIGH:
PRISTINE YOUTH AND FAMILY SOLUTIONS, LLC.
SONS AND DAUGHTERS OF THE MOST HIGH PUBLISHERS ®

OH, GRACIOUS MOST HIGH HEAVENLY FATHER, HOLY IS YOUR
NAME, YOUR WILL BE DONE NOW AND FOREVER!

Love and hate can't dominate the same heart space equally, one will dominate the other as a moral or immoral compass that guides a person's intentions from their heart! That's why when you see the phrase: **"In God We Trust"** on a one-dollar bill, for the children of the devil; this means that money is one of their gods that they love and trust in. Therefore; during an epidemic or during a global pandemic, the children of the Most High always focus on the safety of members of humanity, and always continue to seek refuge in the Most High. The children of the devil always seek refuge in man-made power systems that make money over the public safety of members of humanity, and over human lives. They are guided by their love of money, and desire for man-made power and control!

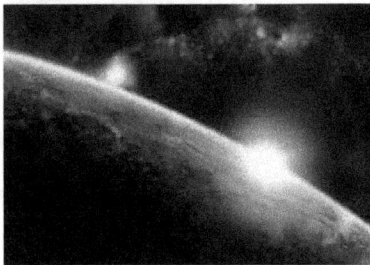

205

CHILDREN OF THE MOST HIGH:
PRISTINE YOUTH AND FAMILY SOLUTIONS, LLC.
SONS AND DAUGHTERS OF THE MOST HIGH PUBLISHERS ®

OH, GRACIOUS MOST HIGH HEAVENLY FATHER, HOLY IS YOUR
NAME, YOUR WILL BE DONE NOW AND FOREVER!

What is money? According the Online American Heritage Dictionary (2020), money is defined as: "A medium that can be exchanged for goods and services and is used as a measure of their values on the market, including among its forms a commodity such as gold, an officially issued coin or note, or a deposit in a checking account or other readily liquefiable account.

What is the purpose of money? On the top front left side of an American $1 bill, it says: "***this note is legal tender for all debts, public and private.***"

206

THE DEVIL IS LUST, LIES, AND DELUSIONS; AND
THE MOST IS LOVE AND TRUTH WITHOUT CONFUSION!

CHILDREN OF THE MOST HIGH:
PRISTINE YOUTH AND FAMILY SOLUTIONS, LLC.
SONS AND DAUGHTERS OF THE MOST HIGH PUBLISHERS ®

OH, GRACIOUS MOST HIGH HEAVENLY FATHER, HOLY IS YOUR
NAME, YOUR WILL BE DONE NOW AND FOREVER!

So, according to the statement on the top front left side of an American $1dollar bill, the **purpose** of having money is **to pay for all debts, public and private**. According the KJV bible book of Ecclesiastics chapter 5 verse 10; it states: "He that loveth _**silver**_ כסף (**Keseph**) **money**) shall not be satisfied with silver כסף (**Keseph**) **money**); nor he that loveth abundance with increase: this is also vanity." **What does this verse mean in the original Aramic (Hebrew) language it was originally revealed in?**

CHILDREN OF THE MOST HIGH:
PRISTINE YOUTH AND FAMILY SOLUTIONS, LLC.
SONS AND DAUGHTERS OF THE MOST HIGH PUBLISHERS ®

OH, GRACIOUS MOST HIGH HEAVENLY FATHER, HOLY IS YOUR
NAME, YOUR WILL BE DONE NOW AND FOREVER!

The original Aramic (Hebrew) word for the translated English word: "loveth or love" is: "אהב" 'âhab 'âhêb, *aw-hab', aw-habe';* אהב is the KJV bible Hebrew Strong's Concordance #**157**. It has a primitive root meaning; to *have affection* for (sexually or otherwise), Usage: to love, (be-) love (-d, -ly, -r), like, friend." He that loveth **silver** (כסף (**keseph**), keh'-sef (**money**); כסף – the word for **silver** is the KJV bible Hebrew Strong's Concordance#**3701**) and means keh'-sef (**money**). In the KJV bible book of **Ecclesiastics chapter 5 verse 10** in other bible translations, it states:

Christian Standard Bible

"The one who loves silver is never satisfied with silver, and whoever loves wealth is never satisfied with income. This too is futile."

Contemporary English Bible Version

"If you love money and wealth, you will never be satisfied with what you have. This doesn't make a bit of sense."

CHILDREN OF THE MOST HIGH:
PRISTINE YOUTH AND FAMILY SOLUTIONS, LLC.
SONS AND DAUGHTERS OF THE MOST HIGH PUBLISHERS ®

OH, GRACIOUS MOST HIGH HEAVENLY FATHER, HOLY IS YOUR
NAME, YOUR WILL BE DONE NOW AND FOREVER!

Good News Translation

"If you love money, you will never be satisfied; if you long to
be rich, you will never get all you want. It is useless." In the
KJV bible book of **1st Timothy chapter 6 verse 10**; it states:
"For *the love of money* is the root of all evil: which while some
coveted after, they have erred from the faith, and pierced
themselves through with many sorrows." **However, it is also
important to be made aware that the lack of money or the
lack of things money can buy, inclusive of health care, can
lead to much preventable suffering.** In the KJV bible book of
1st John chapter 2 verses 15-17; it states: "**Love not the world,
neither the things that are in the world. If any man loves the
world, the love of the** Father **(ELYOWN** עֶלְיוֹן **EL** אֵל**, the
Most High) is not in him**. For all that is in the world, the lust
of the flesh, and the lust of the eyes, and the pride of life, **is not
of the Father (ELYOWN** עֶלְיוֹן **EL** אֵל**, the Most High**), but is
of the world. And the world passeth away, and the lust thereof:
but he that doeth the will of God abideth forever."

209

CHILDREN OF THE MOST HIGH:
PRISTINE YOUTH AND FAMILY SOLUTIONS, LLC.
SONS AND DAUGHTERS OF THE MOST HIGH PUBLISHERS ®

OH, GRACIOUS MOST HIGH HEAVENLY FATHER, HOLY IS YOUR
NAME, YOUR WILL BE DONE NOW AND FOREVER!

So, according to the aforementioned bible verses, if a person loves money, **the love of the Most High Heavenly Father is not in him or her,** and he or she will not ever be satisfied because the love of money is rooted in **the Deadly Venom desire of greed** and greed is unsatisfiable! This is why the **Good News Translation** of the bible says: "If you love money, you will never be satisfied; if you long to be rich, you will never get all you want. It is **useless** (meaning: **futile, pointless, purposeless, impractical, vain, in vain, to no purpose, to no avail, unavailing, hopeless, unusable, ineffectual, fruitless, unprofitable, profitless, unproductive, unachievable**)." A man once stated to **Siddhartha Gautama "Buddha", "I want happiness."** Buddha said, "First remove **"I,"** that's Ego, then remove **"want,"** that's **Desire. See now,** you are left with only "**Happiness.**" Siddhartha Gautama "Buddha" also said: "**Desire is the lead to all suffering.**"

210

CHILDREN OF THE MOST HIGH:
PRISTINE YOUTH AND FAMILY SOLUTIONS, LLC.
SONS AND DAUGHTERS OF THE MOST HIGH PUBLISHERS ®

OH, GRACIOUS MOST HIGH HEAVENLY FATHER, HOLY IS YOUR
NAME, YOUR WILL BE DONE NOW AND FOREVER!

Dr. George Washington Carver said: "We have become ninety-nine percent money mad. The method of living at home modestly and within our income, laying a little by systematically for the proverbial rainy day which is due to come, can almost be listed among the lost arts. How far you go in life depends on your being tender with the young, compassionate with the aged, sympathetic with the striving and tolerant of the weak and strong. Because someday in your life you will have been all of these. There is no short cut to achievement. It is not the style of clothes one wears, neither the kind of automobile one drives, nor the amount of money one has in the bank, that counts. These mean nothing. It is simply service that measures success."

What are some other biblical signs or characteristics of the wicked children of the devil? In the KJV bible book of 2nd Timothy chapter 3 verses 1 through 5; it states: "In the last days perilous times shall come. For [people] (ἄνθρωπος anthrōpos – male and female human beings) shall be lovers of their own selves, covetous, boasters, proud, blasphemers, disobedient to parents, unthankful, unholy, without natural affection, trucebreakers, false accusers, incontinent, fierce, despisers of those that are good, traitors, heady, high-minded, lovers of pleasures more than lovers of God. Having a form of godliness, but denying the power thereof: from such turn away."

211

CHILDREN OF THE MOST HIGH:
PRISTINE YOUTH AND FAMILY SOLUTIONS, LLC.
SONS AND DAUGHTERS OF THE MOST HIGH PUBLISHERS ®

OH, GRACIOUS MOST HIGH HEAVENLY FATHER, HOLY IS YOUR
NAME, YOUR WILL BE DONE NOW AND FOREVER!

In the KJV bible book of Romans chapter 1 verses 18-32; it states: "For the wrath of God is revealed from heaven against all ungodliness and unrighteousness of men, who hold the truth in unrighteousness; Because that which may be known of God is manifest in them; for God hath shewed it unto them. For the invisible things of him from the creation of the world are clearly seen, being understood by the things that are made, even his eternal power and Godhead; so that they are without excuse: Because that, when they knew God, they glorified him not as God, neither were thankful; but became vain in their imaginations, and their foolish heart was darkened. Professing themselves to be wise, they became fools, and changed the glory of the uncorruptible God into an image made like to corruptible man, and to birds, and four-footed beasts, and creeping things. Wherefore, God also gave them up to uncleanness through the **lusts** of their own hearts, to dishonor their own bodies between themselves."

CHILDREN OF THE MOST HIGH:
PRISTINE YOUTH AND FAMILY SOLUTIONS, LLC.
SONS AND DAUGHTERS OF THE MOST HIGH PUBLISHERS ®

OH, GRACIOUS MOST HIGH HEAVENLY FATHER, HOLY IS YOUR
NAME, YOUR WILL BE DONE NOW AND FOREVER!

"Who changed the truth of God into a lie, and worshipped and served the creature more than the Creator, who is blessed forever. Amen. For this cause God gave them up unto vile affections: for even their women did change the natural use into that which is against nature. And likewise, also the men, leaving the natural use of the woman, burned in their **lust** one toward another; men with men working that which is unseemly, and receiving in themselves that recompence of their error which was meet. And even as they did not like to retain God in their knowledge, God gave them over to a reprobate mind, to do those things which are not convenient. Being filled with all unrighteousness, fornication, wickedness, covetousness, maliciousness; full of envy, murder, debate, deceit, malignity; whisperers, backbiters, haters of God, despiteful, proud, boasters, inventors of evil things, disobedient to parents, without understanding, covenant breakers, without natural affection, implacable, unmerciful."

213

CHILDREN OF THE MOST HIGH:
PRISTINE YOUTH AND FAMILY SOLUTIONS, LLC.
SONS AND DAUGHTERS OF THE MOST HIGH PUBLISHERS ®

OH, GRACIOUS MOST HIGH HEAVENLY FATHER, HOLY IS YOUR
NAME, YOUR WILL BE DONE NOW AND FOREVER!

"Who knowing the judgment of God, that they which commit such things are worthy of death, not only do the same, but have pleasure in them that do them." **According to the previous bible verses, the characteristics of the wicked children of the devil are a part of a Lucifer Conspiracy that utilizes lies and fear as a weapon against the children of the Most High**!

Consequently, the messages of the great dragon, called the devil and satan are a part of a **Lucifer Conspiracy**.

CHILDREN OF THE MOST HIGH:
PRISTINE YOUTH AND FAMILY SOLUTIONS, LLC.
SONS AND DAUGHTERS OF THE MOST HIGH PUBLISHERS ℗

OH, GRACIOUS MOST HIGH HEAVENLY FATHER, HOLY IS YOUR
NAME, YOUR WILL BE DONE NOW AND FOREVER!

This **Lucifer** or **Luciferian Conspiracy** has succeeded under the **biblical disguise** of "Leviathan" by inflicting the **spell of Leviathan** which is **another name for the great dragon, that old serpent called the devil and satan** who controls what we see and hear in the media, on television, on the internet, on the radio and on the satellite radio. How? By utilizing what we see and hear in the media, on television, on the internet, on the radio and on the satellite radio to effect members of humanity in four ways:

1. **Meretricious Effect**: Making people unable to see the truth by masking it in lies and deception as apparently attractive, but in reality, having no value or moral integrity.

215

CHILDREN OF THE MOST HIGH:
PRISTINE YOUTH AND FAMILY SOLUTIONS, LLC.
SONS AND DAUGHTERS OF THE MOST HIGH PUBLISHERS ®

OH, GRACIOUS MOST HIGH HEAVENLY FATHER, HOLY IS YOUR
NAME, YOUR WILL BE DONE NOW AND FOREVER!

2. **Death-Dealing Effect**: Capable of causing death as the master orchestrator of chaos, conflict and illusions which causes 100% preventable global confusion amongst members of humanity. **F**aint-hearted **E**xamples **A**mplifying **R**eality **(F.E.A.R.) Effect**. So, always remember that true-faith and trust in the Most High through the True Vine (Yashu'a, Jesus), increases your courage over time. Beware to not **enter fear** in your mind and heart, so that it will not **interfere** with acquiring and sustaining a peace of mind that won't depart; because you are uniquely and wonderfully made, allow the Most High to recreate anew you and don't be afraid!

216

CHILDREN OF THE MOST HIGH:
PRISTINE YOUTH AND FAMILY SOLUTIONS, LLC.
SONS AND DAUGHTERS OF THE MOST HIGH PUBLISHERS ®

OH, GRACIOUS MOST HIGH HEAVENLY FATHER, HOLY IS YOUR
NAME, YOUR WILL BE DONE NOW AND FOREVER!

In the KJV bible book of Revelation chapter 13 verses 15 and 18; it states: "And he had power to give life unto the image of the beast, that the image of the beast should both speak, and cause that as many as would not worship the image of the beast should be killed. Here is wisdom. Let him that hath understanding count the number of **the beast**: for it **is the number of a man**; and his number is **Six hundred threescore and six (666)**."

    3. The **F**aint-hearted **E**xamples **A**mplifying **R**eality (**F.E.A.R**) is strengthened through the **H.O.B.A. effect** which is the **H**abit **o**f **B**eing **A**fraid (**H.O.B.A.**).

> ## The KJV bible book of 2nd Timothy chapter 1 verse 7 states: "For God hath not given us the spirit of fear; but of power, and of love, and of a sound mind."

CHILDREN OF THE MOST HIGH:
PRISTINE YOUTH AND FAMILY SOLUTIONS, LLC.
SONS AND DAUGHTERS OF THE MOST HIGH PUBLISHERS ®

OH, GRACIOUS MOST HIGH HEAVENLY FATHER, HOLY IS YOUR
NAME, YOUR WILL BE DONE NOW AND FOREVER!

4. **Culture Of Accepting Lies (C.O.A.L) Effect**: As the Messiah Yashu'a (Jesus) said: "Ye are of your father the devil, and the lusts of your father ye will do. He was a murderer from the beginning, and abode not in the truth, because there is no truth in him. When he speaketh a lie, he speaketh of his own: for he is a liar, and the father of it."

So, the great dragon, the old serpent called the devil and satan is a liar and a deceiver **who can't ever be trusted!!! How do the children of the Most High overcome fear?** By remembering that real fear is the lack of true-faith, and by remembering that our original purpose in life was and is to gain our way back to our Most high Heavenly Father. **How did we get off the path to the Most High**? We became engrossed in our desires of the things that this physical realm offers more than our desire to obey the Most High. This alone takes us off of the path to the Most High Heavenly One which leads to much preventable **SORROW** and **SUFFERRING** for many of us.

218

CHILDREN OF THE MOST HIGH:
PRISTINE YOUTH AND FAMILY SOLUTIONS, LLC.
SONS AND DAUGHTERS OF THE MOST HIGH PUBLISHERS ®

OH, GRACIOUS MOST HIGH HEAVENLY FATHER, HOLY IS YOUR
NAME, YOUR WILL BE DONE NOW AND FOREVER!

In the KJV bible book of 1st John chapter 1 verses 9-10; it states: "If we confess our sins, he is faithful and just to forgive us our sins, and to cleanse us from all unrighteousness. If we say that we have not sinned, we make him (Yashu'a, Jesus) a liar, and his word is not in us." Therefore; the children of the Most High have an opportunity to repent, to practice the act of doing without doing, to apply ourselves honestly, to put on an incorruptible spirit, and to seek eternal life through the **Messiah Yashu'a (Jesus, Isa, Iesous, Yasue')** by accepting him as our Savior. **Remember: the act of doing without doing does not mean to not have a strong work ethics, and it does not mean to be lazy and do nothing. It means to be at peace while accomplishing the most difficult of tasks and all other tasks every day with maximum effort, skill and efficiency while being in a zone, or only concentrating on the task at hand while simultaneously being in pursuit of becoming an obedient child of the Most High.**

219

THE DEVIL IS LUST, LIES, AND DELUSIONS; AND
THE MOST IS LOVE AND TRUTH WITHOUT CONFUSION!

CHILDREN OF THE MOST HIGH:
PRISTINE YOUTH AND FAMILY SOLUTIONS, LLC.
SONS AND DAUGHTERS OF THE MOST HIGH PUBLISHERS ®

OH, GRACIOUS MOST HIGH HEAVENLY FATHER, HOLY IS YOUR
NAME, YOUR WILL BE DONE NOW AND FOREVER!

What is the Children of the Most High: Pristine Youth and Family Solutions, LLC. Proclamation?

"We greet all in peace with a sincere heart. We are non-violent and agree with the Reverend Dr. Martin Luther King Jr. when he said: "At the center of non-violence stands the principle of love." We stay sober, we don't drink alcohol, we don't become intoxicated, we eat healthy, we exercise, and we don't smoke anything for the body is a temple where the spirit of the Most High dwells; so, our bodies and minds must be in a state of cleanliness! We respect nature, we respect the laws of nature, and the Most High Heavenly Father who is the source of it all. We don't hate any race, creed, religion, or sexual orientation. We advocate that humanity practice being just to the depressed, in mind or circumstances, the poor, and underserved underrepresented members of humanity. We advocate that humanity practice defending the poor, motherless and fatherless from all injustices. We seek to help deliver the poor and needy out of the hands of the wicked by teaching them how to activate the latent potential in them through their inborn gifts, by learning and applying the Most High's doctrine in all that they do, through repentance, and through the acceptance of the Messiah Yashu'a (Jesus), and through the eternal obedience to the Most High Heavenly Father's "Will" and commandments. We seek to help empower members of humanity to take that which is evil and to turn it into good. We seek to work with all members of humanity to help make the world a safer, peaceful, healthy, and poverty free environment for all youth and all adults to live in; and we obey Yashu'a (Jesus) commandment to love one another."

220

CHILDREN OF THE MOST HIGH:
PRISTINE YOUTH AND FAMILY SOLUTIONS, LLC.
SONS AND DAUGHTERS OF THE MOST HIGH PUBLISHERS ®

Oh, children of the Most High make amends with our Heavenly Father if you have not already done so before you take your last breath! Therefore; knowing the aforementioned is essential for those who don't want to be deceived by **the devil's lusts, lies and delusions; but rather acknowledge that the Most High is love and truth without confusion!**

Below is a Prayer of Repentance:

In the KJV bible book of Psalms chapter 51 verses 1-19; it states: "51 Have mercy upon me, O God, according to thy lovingkindness: according unto the multitude of thy tender mercies blot out my transgressions. [2] Wash me throughly from mine iniquity, and cleanse me from my sin. [3] For I acknowledge my transgressions: and my sin is ever before me. [4] Against thee, thee only, have I sinned, and done this evil in thy sight: that thou mightest be justified when thou speakest, and be clear when thou judgest. [5] Behold, I was shapen in iniquity; and in sin did my mother conceive me."

221

CHILDREN OF THE MOST HIGH:
PRISTINE YOUTH AND FAMILY SOLUTIONS, LLC.
SONS AND DAUGHTERS OF THE MOST HIGH PUBLISHERS ®

OH, GRACIOUS MOST HIGH HEAVENLY FATHER, HOLY IS YOUR
NAME, YOUR WILL BE DONE NOW AND FOREVER!

"⁶ Behold, thou desirest truth in the inward parts: and in the hidden part thou shalt make me to know wisdom. ⁷ Purge me with hyssop, and I shall be clean: wash me, and I shall be whiter than snow. ⁸ Make me to hear joy and gladness; that the bones which thou hast broken may rejoice. ⁹ Hide thy face from my sins, and blot out all mine iniquities. ¹⁰ Create in me a clean heart, O God; and renew a right spirit within me. ¹¹ Cast me not away from thy presence; and take not thy holy spirit from me. ¹² Restore unto me the joy of thy salvation; and uphold me with thy free spirit. ¹³ Then will I teach transgressors thy ways; and sinners shall be converted unto thee. ¹⁴ Deliver me from bloodguiltiness, O God, thou God of my salvation: and my tongue shall sing aloud of thy righteousness. ¹⁵ O Lord, open thou my lips; and my mouth shall shew forth thy praise. ¹⁶ For thou desirest not sacrifice; else would I give it: thou delightest not in burnt offering."

222

CHILDREN OF THE MOST HIGH:
PRISTINE YOUTH AND FAMILY SOLUTIONS, LLC.
SONS AND DAUGHTERS OF THE MOST HIGH PUBLISHERS ®

OH, GRACIOUS MOST HIGH HEAVENLY FATHER, HOLY IS YOUR
NAME, YOUR WILL BE DONE NOW AND FOREVER!

"¹⁷ The sacrifices of God are a broken spirit: a broken and a contrite heart, O God, thou wilt not despise. ¹⁸ Do good in thy good pleasure unto Zion: build thou the walls of Jerusalem. ¹⁹ Then shalt thou be pleased with the sacrifices of righteousness, with burnt offering and whole burnt offering: then shall they offer bullocks upon thine altar."

In the KJV bible book of John chapter 14 verse 6; the Messiah Yashu'a (Jesus) said: "I am the way the truth, and the life: no man cometh unto the Father, but by me." However, according to the KJV bible book of John chapter 6 verse 44; only the Most High Heavenly Father can lead a person to the Messiah Yashu'a (Jesus). The Messiah Yashu'a (Jesus) said: "No man [person] can come to me, except the Father which hath sent me draw him: and I will raise him up at the last day."

CHILDREN OF THE MOST HIGH:
PRISTINE YOUTH AND FAMILY SOLUTIONS, LLC.
SONS AND DAUGHTERS OF THE MOST HIGH PUBLISHERS ®

OH, GRACIOUS MOST HIGH HEAVENLY FATHER, HOLY IS YOUR
NAME, YOUR WILL BE DONE NOW AND FOREVER!

In the KJV bible book of John chapter 14 verse 21; the Messiah Yashu'a (Jesus) said: "He **[or she]** that hath my commandments, and keepeth them, he **[or she]** it is that loveth me: and he **[or she]** that loveth me shall be loved of my Father, and I will love him **[or her]**, and will manifest myself to him **[or her]**." All obedient children of the Most High are seeking the Kingdom of God and the Messiah Yashu'a (the True Vine, Jesus), who will take those who have repented, accepted him as their personal savior, and received the holy spirit, to the Most High Heavenly Father. Once a person has accepted the Messiah Yashu'a (Jesus) as their personal savior, there is a Kingdom of God inside of them, but not there exclusively; and they are always being attacked by the children of the devil. "Love gives naught but itself and takes naught but from itself. Love possesses not nor would it be possessed; For love is sufficient unto love." (Gibran, 1968).

224

CHILDREN OF THE MOST HIGH:
PRISTINE YOUTH AND FAMILY SOLUTIONS, LLC.
SONS AND DAUGHTERS OF THE MOST HIGH PUBLISHERS ®

OH, GRACIOUS MOST HIGH HEAVENLY FATHER, HOLY IS YOUR
NAME, YOUR WILL BE DONE NOW AND FOREVER!

In the KJV bible book of Luke chapter 17 verse 21; Yashu'a (Jesus) said: "Neither shall they say, Lo here! or, lo there! for, behold, the kingdom of God is within you."

> "The kingdom of heaven is within you;
> whosoever shall know thyself shall find it."
> Ancient Egyptian Proverb.

In the KJV bible book of Revelation chapter 21 verse 24; it states: "And the nations of those **who are saved** shall walk in its light." So, as living souls, the children of the Most High are made aware that the Supreme Creator of the Boundless Universes; manifests through us as the breath of life, or as the light that shineth in the darkness that the darkness comprehended not!

225

CHILDREN OF THE MOST HIGH:
PRISTINE YOUTH AND FAMILY SOLUTIONS, LLC.
SONS AND DAUGHTERS OF THE MOST HIGH PUBLISHERS ®

OH, GRACIOUS MOST HIGH HEAVENLY FATHER, HOLY IS YOUR
NAME, YOUR WILL BE DONE NOW AND FOREVER!

Therefore, the children of the Most High who are on the **narrow path (which reflects moral integrity and positive character traits in action)** are intentionally, avoiding **the devil's lusts, lies, and delusions** while simultaneously putting our true-faith in the Most High in action; by experiencing that **the Most High is Love and Truth without Confusion!**

226

CHILDREN OF THE MOST HIGH:
PRISTINE YOUTH AND FAMILY SOLUTIONS, LLC.
SONS AND DAUGHTERS OF THE MOST HIGH PUBLISHERS

Appendix

What are the True Vine (Yashu'a, Jesus) Mind Gardening Daily Individual or Family Household Habits of Success? The True Vine (Yashu'a, Jesus) Mind Gardening Daily Individual or Family Household Habits of Success are:

1. **Obey the Most High Heavenly Father's will and commandments now and forever!**

2. **Love the Most High Heavenly Father with all of your heart, all of your spirit, all of your soul, all of your mind, and all of your entire being!**

3. **Decrease so that the Spirit of the Messiah Yashu'a (Jesus) can increase in you!**

4. **Do unto others as you would want others to do unto you!**

5. **Always think positive!**

6. **Always be positive!**

7. **Always have a positive attitude!**

227

THE DEVIL IS LUST, LIES, AND DELUSIONS; AND
THE MOST IS LOVE AND TRUTH WITHOUT CONFUSION!

CHILDREN OF THE MOST HIGH:
PRISTINE YOUTH AND FAMILY SOLUTIONS, LLC.
SONS AND DAUGHTERS OF THE MOST HIGH PUBLISHERS ®

OH, GRACIOUS MOST HIGH HEAVENLY FATHER, HOLY IS YOUR
NAME, YOUR WILL BE DONE NOW AND FOREVER!

8. Open your heart before you open your mouth!

9. Remember, words should be soft, not hard!

10. It's nice to be important, but it is more important to be nice!

11. Mine your mind for the jewels of your soul!

12. Pray together daily!

13. Eat together in the same room a minimum of once a week!

14. Observe the Sabbath (Shu-Bat) weekly as a family!

15. Study and read the scriptures of the Most High as a family a minimum of once a week!

16. Watch a TV show or movie at home a minimum of once a week!

CHILDREN OF THE MOST HIGH:
PRISTINE YOUTH AND FAMILY SOLUTIONS, LLC.
SONS AND DAUGHTERS OF THE MOST HIGH PUBLISHERS ®

OH, GRACIOUS MOST HIGH HEAVENLY FATHER, HOLY IS YOUR
NAME, YOUR WILL BE DONE NOW AND FOREVER!

17. Workout together as a family or ensure that all family members are working out on a weekly basis if their medical physicians have approved of them doing so.

18. Have family meetings once a week to discuss everyone's overall well-being, current events or anything else that is on any family member's mind, without the TV or any other electronic devices being on as a potential conversation distraction. One person speaks at a time, no arguing, no vulgarity, and all family members must respect each other!

19. Do some agreed upon, healthy, fun, and safe family event a minimum of once a month or weekly or bi-weekly together as a family.

229

THE DEVIL IS LUST, LIES, AND DELUSIONS; AND
THE MOST IS LOVE AND TRUTH WITHOUT CONFUSION!

CHILDREN OF THE MOST HIGH:
PRISTINE YOUTH AND FAMILY SOLUTIONS, LLC.
SONS AND DAUGHTERS OF THE MOST HIGH PUBLISHERS ®

OH, GRACIOUS MOST HIGH HEAVENLY FATHER, HOLY IS YOUR
NAME, YOUR WILL BE DONE NOW AND FOREVER!

In the KJV bible book of Genesis, chapter 14 verse 18; it states: "And Melchizedek (Malkiy-Tsedeq, מַלְכִּי־צֶדֶק) king of Salem brought forth bread and wine: and he was the priest of the Most High (ELYOWN עֶלְיוֹן EL אֵל) God." In the KJV bible book of Psalms chapter 82 verse 6; states: "I have said, Ye are gods; and all of you are children of the Most High (is the KJV bible Hebrew Strong's Concordance#5945 which is the title: ELYOWN עֶלְיוֹן (the God) EL אֵל)." In the KJV bible book of Numbers chapter 23 verse 19; states: "God (EL אֵל) is not a man, that he should lie; neither the son of man, that he should repent: hath he said, and shall he not do it? or hath he spoken, and shall he not make it good?" However, for clarification it is critical that all children of the Most High know that in the KJV bible book of Genesis Chapter 1 verse 1; the original Aramic (Hebrew) word for "God" is "Elohiym" not the Most High (ELYOWN עֶלְיוֹן EL אֵל), the Sustainer, the Nourisher, the Provider of all Life, and the Omnipotent and the Omnipresent Creator of the boundless universes. So, the children of the Most High: Pristine Youth and Family Solutions, LLC. hopes that all children of the Most High acquire an overstanding of the differences between "God" ("אֱלֹהִים 'Elohiym") in the KJV bible book of Genesis chapter 1verse 1, "the LORD, יְהֹוָה Yĕhovah, (Yahuwa, Yahweh, Jehovah, Yahayyu)" who repented to the Most High (ELYOWN עֶלְיוֹן EL אֵל) in the KJV bible book of Genesis chapter 6 verse 6; who is referred to as: "the LORD; and the יְהֹוָה Yĕhovah "God" "אֱלֹהִים 'Elohiym" who gets jealous in the KJV bible book of Exodus chapter 20 verse 5; ARE NOT TO BE CONFUSED AS BEING the Most High (ELYOWN עֶלְיוֹן EL אֵל), the Sustainer, the Nourisher, the Provider of all Life, and the Omnipotent and the Omnipresent Creator of the boundless universes who they all worship and do the 'Will" of!

230

CHILDREN OF THE MOST HIGH:
PRISTINE YOUTH AND FAMILY SOLUTIONS, LLC.
SONS AND DAUGHTERS OF THE MOST HIGH PUBLISHERS ®

OH, GRACIOUS MOST HIGH HEAVENLY FATHER, HOLY IS YOUR
NAME, YOUR WILL BE DONE NOW AND FOREVER!

In the KJV bible book of Revelation chapter 11 verses 8-9; it states: "And their dead bodies shall lie in the street of the great city, which spiritually is called Sodom and Egypt, where also our Lord was crucified. And they of the people and kindreds and tongues and nations shall see their dead bodies three days and a half, and **shall not suffer their dead bodies to be put in graves**." In **2020 in the month of April in the state of New York**, due to the thousands of dead bodies of people who died by the hundreds per day from the **Coronavirus (COVID-19)**; the city ordered semi-trucks to stack the bodies as the above verse mentioned "**shall not suffer their dead bodies to be put in graves**." **This is another one of the Yashu'a (Jesus) book of Revelation prophesies fulfilled. What does the KJV bible book of Revelation chapter 11 verse 8 where it states: "And their dead bodies shall lie in the street of the great city, which spiritually is called Sodom and Egypt, where also our Lord was crucified" mean? Meaning, it is taught in this great city that the Messiah Jesus is the Creator (God) and it is taught in this great city that he was crucified on the cross.**

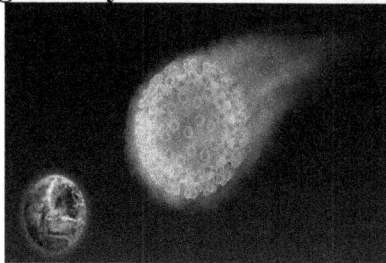

CHILDREN OF THE MOST HIGH:
PRISTINE YOUTH AND FAMILY SOLUTIONS, LLC.
SONS AND DAUGHTERS OF THE MOST HIGH PUBLISHERS ®

OH, GRACIOUS MOST HIGH HEAVENLY FATHER, HOLY IS YOUR
NAME, YOUR WILL BE DONE NOW AND FOREVER!

Nothing would exist if you Oh Gracious Most High Heavenly Father, The Creator didn't create it. You are alone in Your Greatness; you have no partners that share in your grace. To you all sovereignty is due and you are all powerful over everything. We seek refuge in you, the ever watchful Most High who hears and knows all things! Glory be to you as many times as the number of things you have created! All gratitude is due to you oh gracious Most High Heavenly Father, you are the Creator and Sustainer of all the boundless universes. You are the Yielder, and the most Merciful. The Ruler of the Day of Decision. It's you whom we worship and it is you alone whom we beseech for help, oh Guide, guide us to the narrow path (which reflects moral integrity and positive character traits in action) of the ones who stand straight, the narrow path of those who earned your grace not inclusive of those who brought an everlasting curse on themselves, those who conceal the facts of that which they know to be true in order to lead the sincere-hearted seekers of your truth astray. Amen

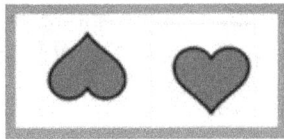

232

THE DEVIL IS LUST, LIES, AND DELUSIONS; AND
THE MOST IS LOVE AND TRUTH WITHOUT CONFUSION!

CHILDREN OF THE MOST HIGH:
PRISTINE YOUTH AND FAMILY SOLUTIONS, LLC.
SONS AND DAUGHTERS OF THE MOST HIGH PUBLISHERS ®

OH, GRACIOUS MOST HIGH HEAVENLY FATHER, HOLY IS YOUR
NAME, YOUR WILL BE DONE NOW AND FOREVER!

About the Author

CHILDREN OF THE MOST HIGH:
PRISTINE YOUTH AND FAMILY SOLUTIONS, LLC.
SONS AND DAUGHTERS OF THE MOST HIGH PUBLISHERS ®

WOODIE HUGHES JR.
CEO & FOUNDER
M.S. & B.S. IN CRIMINAL JUSTICE, ED.D. CANDIDATE

Mr. Hughes is a Servant of the Most High, Teacher of the Most High's Doctrine, and a Youth and Adults Workshop and Presentation Consultant.

📞 478-538-1918
✉ INFO@CHILDRENOFTHEMOSTHIGH.COM
🌐 CHILDRENOFTHEMOSTHIGH.COM
🐦 @WOODIEHUGHESJR9
f CHILDRENOFTHEMOSTHIGHPRISTINEYOUTHANDFAMSOLUTIONS

THE DEVIL IS LUST, LIES, AND DELUSIONS; AND THE MOST IS LOVE AND TRUTH WITHOUT CONFUSION!

CHILDREN OF THE MOST HIGH:
PRISTINE YOUTH AND FAMILY SOLUTIONS, LLC.
SONS AND DAUGHTERS OF THE MOST HIGH PUBLISHERS ®

OH, GRACIOUS MOST HIGH HEAVENLY FATHER, HOLY IS YOUR NAME, YOUR WILL BE DONE NOW AND FOREVER!

Mr. Woodie Hughes Jr. is the CEO & Founder of the Children of the Most High: Pristine Youth and Families Solutions LLC., Sons and Daughters of the Most High Publishers. Mr. Hughes is a Servant of the Most High and a Teacher of the Most High's Doctrine. Mr. Hughes is an Author who writes books that are being put forth by the will of the Most High Heavenly Father to inspire all youth and all adults **who are children of the Most High** to acquire the **competitive edge** against the children of devil. Mr. Hughes is a career university educator. Mr. Woodie Hughes Jr. and Mrs. Tonya Hughes have been happily married for 20 years and have a son and a daughter. Mr. Hughes is a veteran who has received a United States Army honorable discharge for his 8 years of service with the Illinois Army National Guard. **Mr. Hughes is the son of Mrs. Annette Hughes and Mr. Woodie Hughes Sr. who have been happily married for 50 years (as of 2020)!**

234

CHILDREN OF THE MOST HIGH:
PRISTINE YOUTH AND FAMILY SOLUTIONS, LLC.
SONS AND DAUGHTERS OF THE MOST HIGH PUBLISHERS ®

OH, GRACIOUS MOST HIGH HEAVENLY FATHER, HOLY IS YOUR
NAME, YOUR WILL BE DONE NOW AND FOREVER!

For over 27 years, Mr. Woodie Hughes Jr. has continued to be a devout student and teacher of the Most High's doctrine who is guided by the will of the Heavenly Father, and the Messiah Yashua's (Jesus) spirit of knowledge, spirit of wisdom, and spirit of true-faith all working as the same spirits (KJV bible book of 1st Corinthians chapter 12 verses 8-9) of the Messiah Yashu'a (Jesus) which has graciously been bestowed upon him. Mr. Hughes has accepted the Messiah Yashu'a (Jesus) as his savior and is in the Body of Christ!

THE DEVIL IS LUST, LIES, AND DELUSIONS; AND
THE MOST IS LOVE AND TRUTH WITHOUT CONFUSION!

CHILDREN OF THE MOST HIGH:
PRISTINE YOUTH AND FAMILY SOLUTIONS, LLC.
SONS AND DAUGHTERS OF THE MOST HIGH PUBLISHERS ®

OH, GRACIOUS MOST HIGH HEAVENLY FATHER, HOLY IS YOUR
NAME, YOUR WILL BE DONE NOW AND FOREVER!

References

Bergeaud-Blackler, F., Fischer, J., & Lever, J. (Eds.). (2015). Halal matters: Islam, politics and markets in global perspective. Routledge.

Bible, H. (2004). Holman Christian Standard Bible. Nashville: Holman Bible.

Bible, H. (1970). The new American bible. Catholic Bible Publishers. Contemporary English Bible Version.

Carroll, R., & Prickett, S. (Eds.). (2008). The Bible: Authorized King James Version. OUP Oxford.

Gibran, K. (1968). Secrets of the Heart. Hallmark Cards Inc.

Gowan, D. E. (1988). From Eden to Babel: A Commentary on the Book of Genesis 1-11. Wm. B. Eerdmans Publishing.

Hiesberger, J. M. (2006). Catholic Bible. Oxford University Press, USA. Good News Translation.

Houghton Mifflin Company. (2020). Online American Heritage Dictionary. Fifth Edition.

Hughes Jr., Woodie. (2019). Spiritual Trillionaire: Cherishing the Breath of Life While Simultaneously Preparing for the Blow of Death!

THE DEVIL IS LUST, LIES, AND DELUSIONS; AND
THE MOST IS LOVE AND TRUTH WITHOUT CONFUSION!

CHILDREN OF THE MOST HIGH:
PRISTINE YOUTH AND FAMILY SOLUTIONS, LLC.
SONS AND DAUGHTERS OF THE MOST HIGH PUBLISHERS ®

OH, GRACIOUS MOST HIGH HEAVENLY FATHER, HOLY IS YOUR
NAME, YOUR WILL BE DONE NOW AND FOREVER!

References

Kiran C., Chaudhury S. (2009). Understanding Delusions. Ind Psychiatry J. 2009 Jan-Jun; 18(1): 3–18. doi: 10.4103/0972-6748.57851 PMCID: PMC3016695

Lane Arabic/English Lexicon (2003).

Lyubomirsky, S., King, L., & Diener, E. (2005). The benefits of frequent positive affect: Does happiness lead to success? Psychological bulletin, 131(6), 803.

Mayo Clinic (2020) Online Website.

Online Gesenius' Hebrew-Chaldee Lexicon (2020).

Online Merriam-Webster Dictionary (2020).

Online Etymology Dictionary (2020).

Mchie, Benjamin (2019). African American Registry® (the Registry).

Zodhiates, S. (Ed.). (1991). The Hebrew-Greek Key Word Study Bible: King James Version, Zodhaites' Original and Complete System of Bible Study World Bible Publishers, Incorporated.

www.ingramcontent.com/pod-product-compliance
Lightning Source LLC
Chambersburg PA
CBHW060739050426
42449CB00008B/1267